THE CORNUCOPIA

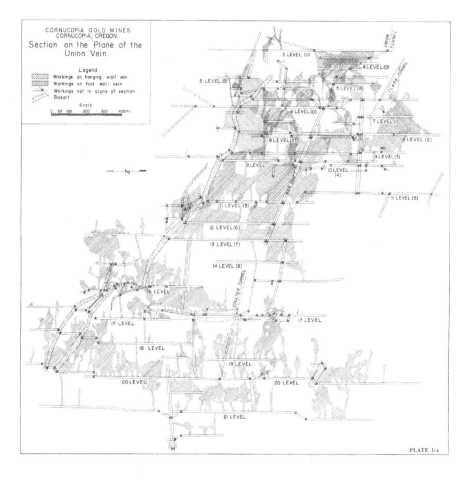

Map of underground workings – Union Mine section of Cornucopia Mines.
Another map details the connected workings of the Last Chance Mine.
USGS, 1968. Public domain.

THE CORNUCOPIA

OREGON'S RICHEST GOLD MINE

Thomas T. Cook

All historical photographs contained in this book are courtesy of the Baker County Library.

ISBN-13: 978-1523330768
ISBN-10: 1523330767

Copyright © 2016 by Thomas T. Cook

Dedicated to the Cornucopia gold miners and their families, Nanci, Eric, Matt and Marge Cook.

Thanks to:

Dale Holcomb, Bonnie Herdlick, Blair Smeddon, Larry Bush, and the Halfway Museum volunteers

CONTENTS

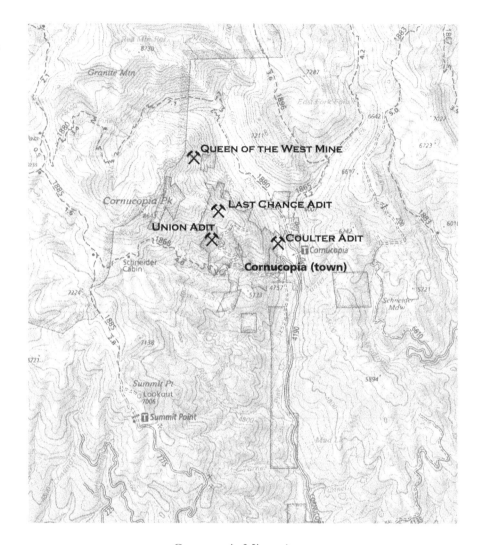

Cornucopia Mines Area
Map location is approximately 12 miles north of town of Halfway.
Base map © GeoGraphics

INTRODUCTION

IN THE RUGGED MOUNTAINS OF NORTHEASTERN OREGON IS A mine, the richest gold mine in the history of Oregon and a ghost town, both named Cornucopia. The mine and town are often thought of as the same entity, they are not. Engineers estimate that there is a vast wealth of gold still buried deep in the ground. Examining the town, before delving into the mine, is pertinent. The earliest site of the town of Cornucopia was located about 1/2 mile downstream, southwest of the southern edge of the existing town site, also on the west side of Pine Creek. Little visible evidence remains at the older town site.

The current mine and town site of Cornucopia sit in a beautiful deep green forested valley. In fall, Aspen leaves glow like flames. The antiquity of the land is visible, a land of towering mountain peaks. Above the mine and town live a few ancient beings; Limber Pine trees who have been here between two and three thousand years. Down near Pine Creek, lately, buildings and foundations survive at the 1890s-to-current town site of Cornucopia. In the ripeness of time, mining towns slip into old age and infirmity. Compared to other gold mining ghost towns, quite a bit remains.

The larger newer town, at its peak size around 1915, consisted of homes and cabins, two hotels (each containing a restaurant and a saloon), six additional saloons, post office, two butcher shops, two general stores, bakery, candy store, post office, school, church, barber shop, two livery stables, jail, one and possibly two houses where one could purchase personal services from sporting women, blacksmith and general repair shop, barber shop, community meeting and dance hall, a small sawmill, and a several mine storage buildings. The management and offices for the Cornucopia Mine, at that time, were up the mountain near the Union mineshaft, part of a huge manager's home called the mansion.

Bootleg whiskey, called 'tangle leg' by Cornucopia gold miners, was popular; regularly made and sold by local moon shiners. Prohibition arrived in Oregon early; 1916. An industry emerged supplying local liquor to thirsty miners and ranchers, and it apparently existed for a while after the end of prohibition in 1933. When prohibition ended, the town enacted an ordinance allowing only beer to be served, no whiskey. One story has a mine mill worker moonlighting as a moonshiner, meaning he distilled illegal whiskey, at the same time he worked at the mill. Moon shiners were sometimes paid in gold flakes and nuggets, somewhat pure gold not smelted from ore, often stolen from the mine. Most miners were sober and hard-working laborers.

Many businesses existed in the town that directly supplied and supported but were not owned by Cornucopia Mines. For example, the mine needed to 800 cords of wood a year in the early years, to fire the boilers that made steam for power and heat. A cord of wood is 4 by 4 by 8 feet, 104 cubic feet of firewood. 800 cords of wood equals 83,200 cubic feet of wood, a humongous pile. Wood needed each year.

At one time there were three tramlines above the town, bringing down ore from high up on Cornucopia Peak down to the Baker mill and hauling up supplies. Just like ski lifts, only with ore buckets instead of chairs. According to *Pine Valley Echoes*, some jobs, such as skilled mechanics to service the tramlines were sometimes in short supply. Another vital town labor need before mechanization took hold in the mid-1920's was the care of horses and repair of wagons. This was, truly, the wild old west.

The landscape of Cornucopia presented a classic second story wooden false front central business district, including a few architectural touches of Victorian elegance. Cornucopia, had the bulk of it survived, could have been used as a movie set. Much of the western movie *Paint Your Wagon* was filmed at a movie company built set near Baker, the closest large town to Cornucopia. The sets were constructed in a mountain meadow not far from Cornucopia. Watching the movie, the temporary movie set town does somewhat resemble the real miner's town. Both towns were largely demolished, one by the movie company, one mainly by snow. The miners probably believed that their town would last a long time. In reality, Cornucopia's existence, like the movie town, proved to be ephemeral.

Cornucopia the town is separated by about three hundred yards from the cluster of ore processing buildings and mine buildings near the 1930's Cornucopia Mine entrance, or adit, called the Coulter. The town is located about two miles down hill from the Cornucopia-Union Mine tunnel, or adit. In 1936 Cornucopia Mines finished blasting and drilled into the heart of the mountain at the lower Coulter adit level, reaching the historic Union and Last Chance mine workings from below. The company built new mill buildings close to the town at this time. By the early1930's, the town of Cornucopia had fallen into serious disrepair, as the mine had greatly reduced payroll and employed far less workers during the 1920's. The mine had shut down altogether for at least two years during the 1920's.

As the price of gold rose, a direct result of an increased level of investment in the mine was that the dilapidated village became occupied and fixed up once again. The boom and bust cycle that is gold mining. In a severe winter, up to 28 feet of snow would fall. An average yearly snowfall of 20 feet would knock down the weaker buildings, unless roofs were cleared of snow. Unoccupied buildings were crushed flat by snow in the space of a few years. A harsh place to eke out a living, this mountain valley.

In Cornucopia town lived hard working families, getting by in a difficult and isolated high altitude environment. For the town's big Labor Day celebration, a rare day off work, miners and town folk had a dance, contests and group games. One game involved two teams of gold miners opposing each other in a tug of war. The miners staked their individual claims, standing in a line on sections of a cleated board, each team holding half of the rope at each end with a red ribbon tied at center. The team that pulled the opposing team past the ribbon won. Another two person gold miner game was a rock drilling contest, one using a hand drill, another using a sledge.

Stories about the struggles and victories of citizens giving this town its heart are told in issues of the local magazine *Pine Valley Echoes*, available at the Halfway Museum. Much is left untold, in this volume, about these brave and intrepid pioneer families. Tempting as it is to tell their tales, our focus is about the mine and miners.

Like the mine, the town died and was reborn several times. So little is now left; it would be a great cultural loss to Oregon if the last few antique buildings in the town fell into ruin. In too short a time a mother lode of Cornucopia Mine history; the last miners who worked the mine, will have vanished. During research efforts for this book, the miner and mine manager's spouse interviewed were 91 and 94. Due to advanced age, citizens of the historic town from the 1930's are now dwindling fast.

Background sources include: miner's stories, state and local archives, newspapers, the detailed collection of official Cornucopia Mine fiscal ledgers at the University of Oregon Library, material from the website of Baker County, interviews at Halfway, and historical records in the author's collection of records from Cornucopia Mine.

Individual mines bought by the company were combined and all named Cornucopia Mines. The corporate entity Cornucopia Gold Mines is not active today. Several well established and profitable mines, the Queen of The West (three miles away) came to be owned by Cornucopia Gold Mines. The mines last produced paying ore under the ownership Cornucopia Gold Mines Company, with company miners and independent lessees working the Union Companion and Last Chance Mines through the Clark and Coulter tunnel entrances. Mine development and exploration work has been done by various owners since mining stopped in 1941.

Cornucopia Gold Mines, at the time of this writing, is owned due to loan defaults, by the General Electric Company: 87 separate claims, approximately one thousand patented acres of land outright, with valid leases on an additional 66 non-patented claims. Expensive mine development work is required to be documented by the government if a company is to hold on to a mineral rights lease on government land that is not patented.

One would assume that a large gold mine with access to two separate rich ore veins, and several other smaller gold bearing veins, would be a rock-solid profit earning business venture. Not so. The vast majority of gold mines in the United States become bankrupt. Gold veins pinch out, labor and development costs constantly rise, owners take too much money out or economic recession causes investors to stop investing money needed for mine operation and development. A labyrinth of possibilities exists for a gold mine to go bust. The pressure of the earth's mantle, the massive shifting of plate tectonics causes rocks to move on their own, as if they are alive.

The mine's fiscal ledger books show that the Cornucopia is truly Oregon's richest mine, occasionally made great profit, also living with the terrible, consistent threat of insolvency. Year after year, the leitmotif reappears in mine records: will the mine survive? It is documented that at least four times Cornucopia Mines has become bankrupt. We know the reasons for the last two times. The mine was not producing and the property tax bills mounted. Records are unclear as to why the mine went bankrupt the first two times. Gold mining is a risky business in so many ways. Cornucopia Mountain hides a wealth of gold. The miners and mountain face each other like adversaries, each of them in a state of change, living men struggling with the living rock. When a miner's soul takes flight from his body, does the mountain's golden heart beat in solemn recognition?

CHAPTER 1
AVALANCHE AND OVERVIEW

IMAGINE STEEP MOUNTAIN CRAGS INTERSPERSED BY SNOW FIELDS. Cornucopia Peak looms up above Pine Valley, bristling with silver grey rock, shining above the snow drifts, like the moon itself. Rain falls on the snow, freezing, then more snow, up to 30 feet deep in drifts, eventually traveling as water down the southern slopes of Oregon's Wallowa Mountains into upper Pine Creek. Water moves on the surface, and directly underground through the rock, through Cornucopia Mine and surrounding creeks, eventually pouring into the Snake River at the mouth of Pine Creek.

Bits and pieces of Cornucopia Peak, with fractured uplifted quartz vein chunks, migrate downstream via the rock falls and avalanches of Pine Creek basin. In ancient times, glaciers scoured the valley. Pieces of gold and gold imbedded in ore, called float by miners, worked free of their vein and appeared miles away from the original source of gold, somewhat like the bundles of D.B. Cooper's hijacking cash found by a boy playing on a beach in the canyon of the nearby Columbia River.

The Snake River canyon, close to Cornucopia, is deeper than the Grand Canyon. Both canyons were carved deep by river erosion. The Snake River canyon, called 'Hells Canyon,' is the deepest river gorge in North America. The canyon walls are about 13 miles east of the Cornucopia Mine the Snake River itself is 17 miles from mine. Its water flows into the Columbia River. The majestic Columbia was followed by Lewis and Clark's Corps of Discovery through the gorge.

Starting at the western edge of the Snake River, the Wallowa Mountains quickly rise up to wild and remote country. Let it suffice to say that all human endeavors: mining towns and camps, gold mines, worker's families, all struggle to survive in the Wallowas. A ten foot wall of flood water once pounded down Pine creek, taking a few people and some of the buildings in the town of Cornucopia with it. Besides floods, avalanches can be deadly, as the following information from a period newspaper article documents.

At an elevation of eight thousand feet, above the town of Cornucopia, above the Queen of the West Mine (later owned by Cornucopia Mines), a snowfield shifted. One layer of the snow pack shifts slightly downward, toward miner Tommy Smith, unheard, unfelt and unseen. The birth of a slab avalanche is a layer of unstable snow with another snow layer on top. The power of deep freezing cold can crack open frozen boulders like cannon shot, and can send tons of snow downhill at breakneck speed.

Underground, hard working miners swing their hammers in cadence. Gold miner Tommy was eating a meal in the cook house outside the mine. In less than a moment, during an odd instant of ominous stillness, from the depth of a gold miner's meal-time daydream, vividly in the here and now, on impulse Tommy reportedly startled before he heard the rumbling.

Could he have known about the avalanche? Was the gold miner at one with the mountain, the snow and the buried stands of White Fir and Lodge Pole on the slopes? As this true tale turns out; Tommy had a heart of gold when facing death.

Simultaneous with the cacophony of trees shattering was the snow's dire rumbling. Cascading shattered snow and ice in motion, a roar like thunder, rolled down the mountain. The avalanche slams into most of the mine surface buildings, smashing them, burying them below the snow with a mix of broken splintered timbers, trees, debris and snow. A catastrophic cement-like wet pile in an instant engulfs him, refuting the miner's futile task of subjugating the earth. Tommy was, perhaps, at one with the mountain's heartbeat when his interior alarm bell rung. Now, the mountain was trying to kill him, trying to still his golden heart.

Tommy was locked in the nightmare state of being buried alive, held immobile in a tomb, and would be for the next six hours. There were other avalanche victims, last year, in the mining basin. Surely Tommy was thinking about last winter when the Superintendent of

Cornucopia Mines, F.C. Dobler, died after being buried alive in a nearby avalanche.

Luckily, there was breathing space in the snow, created by jumbled timbers. At the time, not much was known about avalanche survival. We now know that within 20 minutes, a buried victim develops a fatal ice mask around their face, unless there is amble breathing space. Tommy was pinned fast on the floor of the mess hall by a mixture of heavy timbers and snow. He had ample breathing space, but could neither move hands or feet, with the snow piled nearly 30 feet high above him. It is a miracle that he didn't freeze to death. He was wet, unable to move, and extremely cold. The miners working inside tunnel #5 were saved by simply being inside the mine at the time of the avalanche. The crew was, of course, equipped with shovels. Helped by a supervisor digging towards them from the outside, they were able to quickly dig out of the avalanche covering the mine entrance.

The scene that met them was one of utter devastation. Familiar buildings were gone. Miners who were able to dig uncovered the victims in the bunkhouse, two dead bodies were found there. Two other badly injured bunkhouse miners were put in the unscathed mine office. The survivors, despite some having broken bones, dug in the dark, in a blizzard, to reach the place where they knew the ruins of the mess hall would be. According the *Baker City Herald*, March 14, 1904:

> We finally reached Estes and Tommy Smith in the mess-house. They were pinioned to the floor by heavy timbers and could neither move hands or feet. They were so completely bound down by the timbers that it took more than two hours to release them after we reached them. They had already been there six hours and it is simply miraculous that they had not been killed outright, and that Smith has recovered and that poor Estes lived until the following Saturday.
>
> After we had reached the men and worked for two hours by their silent bodies removing the snow from above the timbers that bound them we found that one large timber laid across Smith's neck at one end while the other end was across the small of Estes' back. These timbers had other timbers on them that extended out into the avalanche. We had to pry the timbers up in order to release the men. While prying at the timber the weight was necessarily increased at one end or the other. When we first began, the weight fell on Smith's neck. This was the first murmur heard. 'Boys, you are killing me,' Smith said calmly.

We then told him of the situation and that one or the other of them must necessarily get a little the worst of it. It did not really look as if we could save one without causing the other's death. We knew they could not last much longer and we had to pry them out at once.

When the matter was explained to Tommy Smith, he bravely said: 'All right, boys, save Estes. He is a married man and it doesn't amount to so much with me.' But we succeeded in getting both the boys out and poor Estes died of his injuries. He was hurt internally.

A primitive kind of medical help was available at the mine office, a 1904 first aid kit. The closest hospital is St. Elizabeth Hospital at Baker, over 50 miles away. According the hospital's 'Our History':

During St. Elizabeth's first year, the sisters provided care to 115 patients, many of them local miners...for a contribution of one dollar a month, each miner received complete health care services...one of the earliest 'Health Maintenance Organizations' in the country.

After World War One, the Cornucopia Mines added a part-time M.D. to the staff, based down the mountain in the town of Halfway. During this winter accident, the hospital in Baker was a full bore day's ride from the mine, partly on a sled-wagon in the snow. That is, if all goes well on the journey. When equipment or horses broke down, the journey to Baker could take two full winter days. Death waited around every bend, as injured miners must have known. For medical help or mine rescue, time is the chief enemy. A critical miner issue in remote villages like Cornucopia is the proximity of medical help. Geography is an important mining issue in several ways.

Although the Cornucopia Mine lies entirely in Baker County, the Union County boundary is 8 miles away. The city of Union is as close as Baker, as the crow flies. Baker is closer, time wise. The old Oregon Trail, going westward toward Baker, passes within 30 miles of Cornucopia. Until a newer road was built, when ambulance wagons rolled down from Cornucopia towards Baker, they followed, for a short while, the actual ruts of the Oregon Trail on Flagstaff Hill. Baker was still a tiny hamlet when the last pioneer wagons rolled along the Oregon Trail. Later, when a hospital was first built at Baker, numerous gold miner and rancher lives were saved.

Miners on Tommy's team considered themselves lucky, after seeing the devastation of the avalanche. It's likely they thanked God to be alive.

Some Cornucopia miners had strong spiritual leanings. Working inside the earth includes a spiritual aspect, as any work can. While working underground, the earth can speak directly to your ears; crackling, dripping and creaking. Visually, one can encounter wondrous beauty inside a mine. Spiritual beauty can be manifested as a mundane but intricate mixture of bright rock colors, but rarely the lusty gleam of gold. There can be deeper meanings that co-exist with the quest for gold, for example, the quest for spirit.

The day of the avalanche, mother earth was kind to some of the crew. For unlucky miners, mother earth can be mother death. Cave-ins also took the lives of a few Cornucopia miners with sudden fatal rock-fall. Mountains of rock formed during cataclysmic eruptions, naked rock, ancient rock, tricky rock, silent rock, whispering rock, worthless rock, and some rocks that had gold inside. Gold ore often is streaked brown, oxidized by carbolic acid from water seeping downward, or gray sulphide ore, or mysterious oxides and tellurides. Larger mines use a geologically trained engineer on staff. The engineers, as supervisors, direct the crews where to excavate. The mining crew has to fight the rock to get it to reveal its buried treasure.

Local workers, plus Cornish and Scandinavian miners worked the Cornucopia. Smith's fellow crew members, miners such as Nils Lundstrom, saved his life. The Cornish miners held old mine traditions and superstitions from southwest England. To them, ghost Tommy Knockers exist, and are real. According to Cornish lore, if you were kind to your brother miners, the Tommy's would let you know by knocking a warning before a cave-in happened. If you didn't listen carefully for the knockers, or if they didn't knock, the mine could be your tomb. Miner's efforts at controlling the earth often backfired. Any ally, fictional or not, is of assistance.

Ghosts could be personal, for perhaps the place they haunt is oneself. Incidents occur; accidents develop for mysterious reasons in this remote part of Oregon. The work of a gold miner might seem routine from the view of a non-miner. In reality it is anything but routine. At the time of this accident, the Union-Companion Mine and The Queen Mine were owned by different companies. In a disaster like this, all the miners worked together, no matter which mine they worked for.

Union-Companion Mine was the largest of the mines, including

Queen of the West, that eventually were all named Cornucopia Mines. The word Cornucopia derives from the Latin words for horn of plenty. Other Cornucopia named mines, not related to Oregon's, exist in Arizona and Nevada. According to *Oregon Geographic Names*, Cornucopia, a mining camp at the time, was first named in 1885 by unknown miners from Cornucopia, Nevada.

The original Union Mine, and most other mines in the Cornucopia area were eventually consolidated under the ownership of Cornucopia Mines. Besides the mining village of Cornucopia, the nearest town of any size is Halfway. Cornucopia town was often called 'Copia' by the miners. Halfway, now the largest town in the immediate area, was so named because it was halfway between the town of Cornucopia and the now nearly vanished town of Pine Valley.

Gold was first discovered in Baker County, west of Baker City, in 1861. The largest single pure piece of gold ever found in the area is called the Armstrong Nugget. The nugget is on display at the U.S. Bank in Baker. It weighs 80 ounces, and rounding up the value of gold to $2,000 an ounce, the big nugget would be worth close to $200,000. To collectors, large chunks of gold are worth more than their aggregate weight. Near Cornucopia, gold was found in Sparta in 1863, then at Cornucopia in 1880. It is a matter historical dispute as to who first found gold at Cornucopia. One source states that the Union Mine was one of the first to be located in the area, and it was first claimed by Clint Dilley, Wash Tice, Bill Burdette and Fred Huntington in 1884. The mine was named after the Civil War notion of Union. The Union Mine had obvious influence from the nearby Union County and city.

The Union Mine's immediate neighbor mines were named: Companion, Last Chance, Clark, Queen of the West, Whitman, Red Jacket, Mother Lode and Mayflower, all in Baker County. Both the Union Mine, Union County and Baker City names have Civil War origins. Cornucopia was connected to towns by stage coach roads. For as long as stage coaches operated, two stages arrived at Cornucopia each day. One was the stage from the northwest, from Union, and one from Baker, to the southwest. The stages brought, as you can imagine, all kinds of goods and people to the little mountain boom town of Cornucopia.

What form of battle would occur if a team of Dixie singing southern miners accidentally broke through the wall of a mine stope into a neighboring mine worked by Union army sympathizers? The Union army veteran's group "Grand Army of the Republic" Joe Hooker Post #20 was active in Union County until the 1930's. Ghosts of the Civil War could be easily rekindled. At the time of the avalanche described, the Civil War was just 39 years in the past.

The city and county of Baker were named after Edward Baker, one of the first two Senators from Oregon, a close friend and former law partner of Abraham Lincoln.[1] Baker was appointed Oregon's U.S. Senator and then given a commission as a Colonel in the Union Army. Before the Civil War, Abraham and Mary named their second child Edward, after Edward Baker of Oregon. Baker was killed early in the war in the 1861 battle of Ball's Bluff, after spending the previous day at the White House with Lincoln and his sons. Lincoln was brought to tears by his friend Baker's death. Baker was indeed an Oregon patriot. Baker was the only member of the United States Congress to die in the Civil War. In 1862, Baker County was created in his honor, taken from part of what was the larger Wasco County.

Earlier, according to Oregon Historical Society, Abraham Lincoln had been offered the governorship of Oregon Territory, and declined the offer. The state of Oregon and Baker County contain Civil War roots.

The Civil War was also fought, in small ways, in the old west. There were small battles as far west as New Mexico. Strong feelings existed for each side throughout Oregon. West of the town and mine named Union was the then booming gold mine town of Sumpter. According to the Cracker Creek Museum of Mining, Sumpter was likely named by "five Confederate soldiers on their way to the California gold fields." Obviously, the town of Union was known to be town of Union cause sympathizers. Between Sumter and Union was La Grande, which had some Southern sympathizers, in addition to La Grande's Union sympathizers. West of Sumter, a Dixie Creek mining district, north of Prairie City, was dominated by Southern sympathizers.

Soon after Lincoln's 1864 reelection, some pro-Confederate citizens, ranchers and miners at La Grande decided to erect an effigy of Lincoln in the center of the town, and burn it in a public ceremony.[2] Pro-Union townspeople, believing that a rebellious act of perfidy might soon occur, quickly rode to the mining town of Union and gathered a militia group to help them prevent the burning of the Lincoln effigy.

Shades of Paul Revere, the motley Union de-facto militia quickly rode back to La Grande. Before the effigy torching time arrived, word reached the would-be pro-Confederate militia in La Grande that the larger pro-Union militia was nearby. It is rumored that some drinking was going on prior to the scheduled burning. Not just a burning-man effigy, but the image the United States itself was at stake.

Arming themselves, Southern sympathizers hid under wagons and behind bushes in the vicinity of the effigy. Battle was a distinct possibility. When the obviously larger and better armed pro-Union group arrived, the Union militia leader stood in front of the effigy and let it be known that whoever dared torch the (probably ugly version of Lincoln) effigy would suffer immediate and grievous harm. The Lincoln was not burned. Reportedly, no gunfire erupted. Unfortunately, no photographs survive of the effigy. The effigy had to have included a makeshift stovepipe hat, perhaps clothed in an American flag? Or, sensibly, the unburned Lincoln effigy was likely wearing worn out gold miner's clothes blacked with soot to resemble a suit. Mining companies, no matter how large, did not fund clothing for miners. Clothes were an expensive necessity for miners in the frontier, especially those who worked for the many, low wage, small mines predominating in the area.

Cornucopia Mines was once counted among the six largest mines in the entire United States. The Cornucopia group of mines, including the Union Mine, Clark Mine, Last Chance Mine and Coulter adit, operated from 1884 to 1941, with a period of shut down from 1927 to 1929. The shut down did not correspond with the great depression. Yet, the economy of mining is affected by nation-wide economic, population, even political trends.

The population of Baker County, by 1880, stood at six and one half thousand. Baker County, at that time, included what is now Wallowa County. By 1900, the county population was approximately 16,000. This figure does not include any of the few remaining tribal members of iconic Native American Chief Joseph's tribe; as Wallowa County had, by then, been separated from Baker County.

Agriculture, then mining, were the primary industries of Union and Baker County during that period of population growth. Throughout the west, despite the gold and silver rushes, agriculture has produced more wealth than mining. Timber was a distant third at the time. By 1960, the population of Baker County had grown to just 18,000. In the sixty years between 1900 and 1960, the entire population of the county had grown by just 2,000. Once mining and ranching were established, few new jobs were created.

The latest census gives Baker County a population of 24,000. According to the Atlas of Oregon, ranching and mining were the primary engines of population growth in Baker County, ranching more than mining.[3] By the 1950's, timber took the place of mining as an economic engine.

How is it possible to economically measure what is largely hidden from view? Records specific to individual gold mines are difficult and often impossible to locate. Mines had investor and business competition reasons to shield records of their production from public view. The business history of Cornucopia Mines is detailed in chapter three. Much of the mine income was earned before there was a federal or state corporate tax structure, few mine records exist prior to 1918. Businesses in Oregon started paying income tax during World War One. Governmental records documented business growth and decline. There are other ways to measure the mine's fiscal health. For example, population data shows a strong correlation, in earlier times, between the growth of Cornucopia Mines, as it became the largest mine in the region, and the growth of population in Baker County.

Different methods exist, of course, besides mine production or census, to measure riches. The Wallowa Mountains region is known as Oregon's "Little Switzerland." One of the mountains in the range is called the Matterhorn. The Wallowa Mountains have been recognized as one the most beautiful parts of Oregon. These mountains are a place of stunning natural beauty, with or without settlers. The history of white settlers in the Wallowas, of course, represents a fraction of the scope of human habitation at sites like Cornucopia.

---

[1] "History of Baker County, Oregon," Baker County Historical Society, from Historical Society official website.

[2] *Illustrated History of Union and Wallowa Counties*, Western Historical Publishing Co. 1902.

[3] Loy, William G., Stuart Allan, Aileen R. Buckley and James E. Meacham, *Atlas of Oregon*. Second Edition, Eugene: University of Oregon Press, 2001, page 11.

CHAPTER 2

CORNUCOPIA'S ORIGINAL OWNERS

"The earth is our mother. She should not be disturbed by hoe or plough....white men had found gold in the mountains around the land of the winding water...{you must} understand fully with reference to my affection for the land. I never said the land was mine to do with as I choose. The one who has a right to dispose of it is the one who has created it."

THESE ARE WORDS FROM NEZ PERCE CHIEF JOSEPH.[4] THE NEZ PERCE were driven out of the Wallowa Mountains and were in the process of being forced onto a distant reservation in Idaho when they decided to flee the U. S. Cavalry. The same story of being cheated out of their lands, the story of many tribal-government interactions in Oregon, told throughout the United States.

Joseph's protracted flight from the U.S. Cavalry, when he attempted to take refuge in Canada with what was left of his tribe, is well documented. The Nez Perce occupied this beautiful corner of Oregon long before the gold miners and settlers. Of course, Native Americans have inhabited Oregon for thousands of years. The Nez Perce people were the tribe that ensured Lewis and Clarke's survival by supplying them with horses, when the pace of the Corps of Discovery's slow walk through the mountains in winter would have probably resulted in starvation.

Today, the bulk of the Nez Pierce tribe resides in Idaho about 80 miles northeast of the Cornucopia area. The west is not as vast as it appears, map wise. There is a corner of Montana, 150 miles from Cornucopia, once occupied by the Nez Perces.

During early interactions between Native Americans and settlers, there were atrocities on both sides. The Whitman massacre is a nationally known example of Native American violence towards missionaries. There are comparable examples, in Oregon, of white violence toward Native Americans. For example, not far from the Whitman site, a few years later, the Walla Walla chief Peopeo Moxmox approached United States troops under a white flag of truce, wanting to discuss several issues. He was taken prisoner. In captivity, he was later butchered and dissected, and his entire parley party was killed.

The Nez Perces had nothing to do with the Whitman Mission massacre incident. For the most part, the Nez Perce tribe helped white refugees from the Whitman massacre survive until U. S. troops arrived. Alvin Josephy Jr.'s book *The Nez Perce* documents these incidents in careful detail, also how an invasion of gold miners in the 1850's was the primary reason that the Nez Perce, the Umatilla and other local tribes lost the vast majority of their lands.[5]

Lewis and Clark, the Nez Perce tribe and the Whitman incident all loom large in the history of north-eastern Oregon. So far, documentation has not been found regarding any direct connection between the Nez Perce, Umatilla or the Walla Walla tribes and Cornucopia. Obsidian arrowheads have been found by locals in the Cornucopia area. At one time there was a mine near the Cornucopia Mine called the Whitman. The author could locate no Cornucopia area gold mines named after Native Americans.

Like the Nez Perce, the Walla Walla and Umatilla tribes of the Southern Plateau visited the forests and meadows in Pine Valley, including the Cornucopia Mine area, at various times. Heavy snows kept the area from year round tribal habitation. The Cornucopia area was used as a summer hunting ground. The Atlas of Oregon shows Pine Creek Valley and the Cornucopia area as the border between Nez Perce and combined Walla Walla, Cayuse and Umatilla tribal lands. The primary reason Native Americans were driven from this area, according to several historical sources, is simply put: gold miners and timber companies wanted it.

Miners sometimes called natives, with a negative connotation, 'sheep eaters,' due to Mountain Goat and Bighorn Sheep being a part of their diet. The term sheep eaters was used in a non-flattering way. The term has been used in western literature as early as the 1860's and in other states. Native Americans wondered why the gold miners were tearing up the earth and polluting the streams. How would their tribe have enough dried winter food to survive, when deer and wild sheep were scarce and fish disappeared from the streams? Even worse, white traders accompanying the miners brought whiskey for trade. These traders would cheat natives out of their furs, giving them cheap whiskey in return. Relations were often sour between traders, miners and natives. To some, Pine Valley did not have a particularly spiritual or cultural aspect; it was just a high mountain valley where money could be made.

Pine Valley is contained by current Baker County, including the Cornucopia Mine area. Charles Fee was the first settler to have recorded interactions with the Native Americans. Fee came to Pine Valley to trap beaver in the 1850's, settling in Pine Valley around 1860. Dunham Wright, who passed through the valley in 1862 with a wagon train, said Fee was still the only pioneer living in Pine Valley. Fee was well known for positive and helpful relations with neighboring Native Americans, taking injured natives in his wagon to Baker for medical treatment. Fee was known to be a friend of the Umatilla Chief Black Hawk and the Nez Perce tribe.[6]

Chief Joseph's father, Old Joseph, purportedly affixed his X on a peace treaty in 1855, allowing his people to retain 7.6 million acres of their traditional lands in the northern Wallowa Mountains, although the 1855 treaty took away the area surrounding Cornucopia Mines from the tribe. An 1863 treaty, following the first onslaught of gold seekers into north-eastern Oregon, greatly reduced the quantity of Native American land to 1.1 million acres. Old Joseph believed the 1863 treaty was never ratified by his people.[7] Old Joseph was outraged that the federal government took back nearly six million acres of their land, after promising it to his people.

What was eventually proposed by the U.S. was even worse to the Nez Perce in particular. The Native Americans were ordered to leave the Wallowas permanently and move to a reservation already occupied and crowded by other Nez Perce bands in present day Idaho. The Idaho Nez Perce bands had a history of treaty negotiation with the government. The 1863 reservation was one tenth the size of their former lands, already greatly reduced in size. When this governmental reneging was first related to Old Joseph, he burned his American flag and bible, remaining totally resistant to the white man's plans until his death in 1871. His son became chief. Due to the Civil War, federal treaty enforcement of the disputed 1863 agreement was delayed. An onslaught of miners moved onto Nez Perce land during the Civil War.

Joseph's people's rights, or deed to live throughout the Wallowa Mountains dates from the 1855 treaty. A few white settlers and gold seekers had begun moving into the area in the 1850's. In 1850 Congress passed the Donation Land Law. This law granted previously occupied Native American lands to white or Indians of mixed blood, provided they were United States citizens or would become citizens within a year. At the time, full-blood Native Americans were denied U. S. citizenship. The 1855 treaty stated that the government would allow no white settlers within reservation boundaries. This agreement was rarely, if ever, enforced by the government.

Settlers wishing to obtain nearly free land from the government had to agree to stay on the land for four years. Each couple received 320 acres for a nominal fee. If single, a settler was required to marry one · year after arrival. The settlers needed to immigrate to Oregon between December 1850 and December of 1855. Settlers could purchase their claim for $1.25 per acre after two years of successive residence on the land. The U.S. government's Homestead Act of 1862, signed by Abraham Lincoln, further eroded Native American lands.

An 1873 treaty signed by President Grant seemed to again affirm the Nez Perce's ownership of much of the northern part of the Wallowa Mountains. This treaty did not include Pine Valley, to the south, as Native American territory. In 1875 the 1873 agreement with the Indians was revoked without compensation. Wallowa Valley and the surrounding mountains suddenly became public land available for mining and settlement. By the late 1870's there were few Nez Perces remaining in the Wallowas.

Joseph and his band, avoiding ruinous battles with the much better equipped U.S. Cavalry, nearly succeeded in fleeing with their lives to refuge, almost to the Canadian border. After what is considered an ambush during which many natives of all ages were killed, and supplies destroyed, Joseph surrendered and gave his famous "Fight No More" speech. Civil War veteran General Howard was the leader of the Army, he had lost an arm in the Civil War, and was called 'one arm' by the natives. Howard eventually captured Joseph and his people, refusing to allow the band to return even to their relatives in Idaho. The band, years later, was eventually allowed to resettle with relatives on the Nez Perce reservation in Idaho.

The Native American's land became public land. In many instances, pioneers, ranchers and farmers developed legitimate government claims, a few remain in the same honest family's possession to this day. In other instances, large corporations bought up vast tracts of combined individual land claims that were, initially and then in aggregate, totally spurious.

A 1908 book *Looters of the Public Domain* written by S.A. Puter and Horace Stevens (formerly a U.S. Land Office official) and published by Portland Press, presents 495 single spaced small font pages of specific examples of documented land fraud in Oregon. Puter wrote the book from his jail cell, convicted of land fraud against both natives and settlers. The book lists exhaustive, detailed research on a litany of large scale land thefts and graft. Names of private corporation officers, corrupt government officials, their judicial trials and either rare convictions or 'get out of jail free' examples are listed in detail in the book. Oregon laws were later enacted to stem the tide of looting, in part as a result of this book's publication. According to Puter, most of the private corporate officers who bought land claims, coming from out of state to begin with, sold their ill-gotten land and had ample time to flee the state with their bags of gold and notes, before they could be prosecuted.

---

[4] *The Nez Perce Indians.* Alvin M. Josephy Jr. Mariner Books, 1965.

[5] *The Nez Perce Indians.* Alvin M. Josephy Jr. Mariner Books, 1965, page 356.

[6] *Chief Joseph: The Biography of a Great Indian,* Chester Anders Fee, Wilson-Erickson, 1936.

[7] Source from: www.pbs.org/weta/thewest/resources/archives (episode #4).

CHAPTER 3

MINE, METHODS, MONEYMEN AND MINERS

CORNUCOPIA MINE IS INDISPUTABLY THE HIGHEST PRODUCTION gold mine in Oregon's history. One nickname for the mine was "The El Dorado of Eastern Oregon." Government estimates of Cornucopia Mine total income from the 1880's through 1941 are as high as $20,000,000.[8] This estimate values gold at about one quarter of what it is worth today. There is another government record total production estimate of $10,000,000 and another figure quoted at $15,000,000. Using the lowest of the figures, Cornucopia still stands as the most productive gold mine in Oregon's history. These figures include a small percentage of value derived from silver, lead and other metals recovered during the gold smelting process.

Total output of the mine in current dollars, if gold is valued at close to $1,000 + an ounce, would be closer to $50,000,000.+ If an expensive spur railroad had been funded to provide access directly to the mine, Cornucopia Mine would have been far more profitable than it was. Mine profit is affected by transportation costs, quality of management, labor, exact engineering, ore processing efficiency and luck.

The universe of gold mining is divided into two worlds, placer and lode. Placer mining is basically surface area mining. In the old west, placer mining often meant a solitary miner with a gold pan, a wooden rocker or a sluice box to wash the soil and debris away from the gold nuggets. The smaller flecks of 'free' placer gold then had to be separated from a black sand mix. If available, mercury was added to the mixture, which forms an amalgam of mercury and gold. The mercury is then evaporated from the amalgam with fire, leaving just the gold.

. Another type of placer mining, always environmentally destructive, was to totally divert the stream water, sifting the entire surface area and washing for gold. This often involved digging down into the old stream bed several feet, blasting boulders, generally wreaking havoc on the river bed and surrounding riparian vegetation.

Placer mining devolved into even more destructive methods: hydraulic and dredge mining. Hydraulic mining, banned in California and Oregon starting in 1884, used industrial high volume pressure water hoses, like large fire hoses, to erode away stream banks and expose ore. Dredge mining involved the process of damming and flooding a valley, then setting up a large flat bottomed boat with a dredge on it to sift through all the surface material in the valley. One can still see the tailings piles of dredge mining in valleys like Sumpter, mile after mile of bare rock piles.

Much of the Sumpter Valley was stripped of top soil and vegetation in the process. Another method of placer mining was to use a drag line and bucket attached to a crane, also stripping all the soil, rocks and vegetation to sift for gold. These were legal and accepted mining practices at the time.

Lode mining involves digging into the earth, sometimes at the place where the gold vein surfaces, sometimes going deep before reaching a gold vein. There is an Edgar Allan Poe quality to a lode mine; a dark tomblike place. A lode is defined as a vein that contains metals. Ore veins usually run at an angle, not straight up or down. The veins bulge in width, then pinch out to nothing, then sometimes resume lower down. The hanging wall is the ground being mined overhead, the footwall going down. Steep vein angles increase production costs.

Mining profit, or loss, is always affected by technology. In the 1880's when the Cornucopia area was first mined, dynamite was newly introduced in mines. Previously, black powder had been used, four times less explosive that the same amount of dynamite, with much more toxic smoke.

The Cornucopia, always a 'lode' mine, fought for its fiscal survival against far more environmentally destructive and yet less expensive and less technical placer methods of mining, still winning the fiscal battle for highest individual company gold production.

Four boxes of records from Cornucopia Mines have been thankfully saved: two at the University of Oregon Knight Library and at two at the University of Utah Marriott Library. Interestingly, the corporate mine records are preserved courtesy of the corporate generosity of Nike and Marriott. The University of Oregon collection includes the time period: 1918-1921 (few records), and a fairly complete picture of the fiscal records of the mine from 1922 to 1941. Mine records from both periods indicate that the mine owners and managers had a social conscience, in addition to profit motives.

A multi-page section in Cornucopia mine records is labeled "Civic Welfare." The ledger entries include: paying doctor's and teacher's salaries, lumber, supplies and a telephone line for the school, miner's medical expenses at St. Elizabeth Hospital. During World War One, substantial corporate donations were made by the mine to Red Cross and Salvation Army. The mine bought, during that period, $2,000 worth of U.S. patriotic savings bonds. The corporation, even though occasionally teetering on the edge of fiscal ruin, still demonstrated a kind heart. For what could be viewed as, but are not necessarily selfish reasons, the mine funded the growth of the infrastructure of the town of Cornucopia.

Numerous bills in the file, over the years, were paid by the mine for: pipes and plumbers to install and maintain a civic water system, electric wire and electricians for power from their power house on Pine Creek to the town's buildings. There are no entries in accounts receivable for any charges to the citizens of Cornucopia for home electricity or water, so it is possible that water and power were free to town citizens. The mine also paid for building the town's large dance hall, as related by miner Chris Schneider, and funded community meals during celebrations.

Contrary to the hit song about miners owing their souls to (a heartless) company store; during three different years the Cornucopia Mines owned dry goods store, supplying miners with clothes and other needs, the company store lost several hundred dollars at the end of each year. The company store certainly was not heartless. When the entire year's income was compared to expenses, the store deficit was written off as an expense against taxes. During 1922, the ledgers indicate that the company store lost $388 for the year. Two other years indicate smaller losses. Mine owners do not normally fund money losing operations. The owners of Cornucopia did.

The ledgers provide insight into how the mine was run, and the expense of goods and services in the remote mountains of Oregon, before and during the depression. The one telephone line from the nearest town Halfway to the mine office averaged a total cost of $110 per month from the late 1920's to the 1940's. The mine-paid telephone line bill alone added up to a large expense during hard economic times. Numerous entries, over the years, detail the mine paying expensive bills for: drills, explosives, cyanide, timber and lumber, firewood, pipes and fittings, machine parts, tools, steel cable, machines, iron stock, lubricants, oil, coal, lime, lighting supplies, building materials, food for the boarding house, and massive amounts of money paid in wages to managers, miners, subcontractors and other workers.

Underground expenses in the Cornucopia ledgers were coded, up until the late 1930's, with a 'U' for Union mine and an 'L' for Last Chance mine, even though the two mines were connected by an underground drift. No expense records could be found for the Queen of the West mine, although the company owned that mine. It is likely that no mining work was done at the Queen of the West from the early 1920's on. The mine was several miles - more - away from Cornucopia's Mine mill site, and thus more expensive to operate. One reference was found that indicated that some of the Queen of the West ore dump was trucked down to the Baker Mill to be reprocessed.

Mine expenses were divided up into separate categories: mining, assay office, milling, surface expense, production, compression {air}, stables, blacksmith shop, boarding house, power house, legal and marketing. Marketing category referred to out of state ore refining expenses, not as we currently think of it

There were at least three separate mine mills built. The old mills were inefficient, newer technology was used in the 1930's ore mill at the Coulter adit.[9] In 1919, the Union Mine mill had a stable, with accompanying expenses. In 1920, the company paid for 216 cords of wood, and a large amount of coal. Bills exist from the Pacific Seafood Co. for large quantities of fish -mainly salmon. There is record of paying wages for a milker, also in 1920, at the Union Mine stable. Other records exist detailing the company's efforts at making sure the miners were well fed with healthy food. These are numerous expenses the mine did not have to provide, as miners could buy groceries from private grocery stores, at the time, in Cornucopia or Halfway.

The mine owners could have provided canned milk at the mine boarding house, instead of the fresh milk. The records are incomplete; some ledgers are missing from the 1930's decade. I could find no records of any medical expenses except for bills paid to the hospital in Baker, as one example.

After all mine bills were paid, profits were invested. The mine invested in several ways. For example, between 1919 and 1926 the mine received $414,000 income from previously purchased U.S. Treasury bonds. These profits helped the mine survive during the fiscally difficult (for gold mines) late 1920's. The mine manager knew how to invest profits wisely.

The highest individual expense, over several years, appears to be money paid to the manager, Robert M. Betts. This may appear suspect, but he was the primary investor at the time. Robert Betts was raised in a mining family, his father was involved in mining in Spokane, WA. Later the Cornucopia Mines Co. headquarters would be located in Spokane. Betts first appears in the records as a mine engineer for Cornucopia Mines is 1916. Betts was listed as a board member of the Oregon State Board of Examiners for Engineering from 1929 to 1937. He last appears in the records as a board member in 1937.

Once Betts ascended to management/ownership, his risky investment started to pay off. According to a mine journal entry, in 1927 he personally invested $200,000 in the just bankrupt and then newly incorporated mine. He may have invested even more money in the mine earlier, but existing ledgers do not show it. These investments were a gigantic fiscal exposure for Betts, for stock owners can be assessed fees for mine repairs. There is no guarantee of profit in the mining business.

Mine payments made to Betts, during the period 1927 to the mid-1930's, beside his $750 monthly salary to manage the mine, totaled $766,000. This amount was paid to him in installments and stock dividends. There is record, in 1935, of a special committee of board members formed to determine how much to compensate Betts. The total compensation for Betts represents a three and one half times return on his initial investment, albeit over a long period of time. Betts was a high stakes gambler, and he won.

In 1934, the mine sent notices to shareholders demanding that they sell their shares. A "Certificate of decrease in capitol stock in the state of Oregon" was filed. Betts sold most of his shares in 1934, as did most of the shareholders. Large shareholders Lester G. Kaas and Lewis R. Morris bought into the new corporation and controlled approximately 200,000 shares between them. All other shareholders individually owned less than 15,000 shares each. Betts and two of his family members continued on the Board of Directors.

By 1935 the new corporation had all assets and stock transferred to "Cornucopia Mines Corporation" based in Spokane. Stock was again issued, likely to pay for the new expensive two miles long 'Coulter' tunnel and new mill, down at the level of the town of Cornucopia. A Cornucopia corporate manager in Seattle, also a stock investor, was named A.D. Coulter. Incredibly, records show that the mine was sold, at that time, to the new Spokane based corporation for $125,000. This seems to be a bargain price. There may have been new company stock shares given to the old stock holders in the new company, but that is not documented.

Many of the records stored at the University of Oregon Library are legalistic documents having to do with compliance with Oregon's incorporation laws, expenses, worker's compensation insurance and stock ownership. Several reports list and name individual stockholders, numbering 50 investors on average each report. This small figure indicates a closely held corporation of stockholders who could, at various times, meet and possibly influence the direction of the mine. The longest tenured president of the board of directors was Betts.

One report has Betts owning over 4,000 preferred shares and 2,500 common shares, and the rest of the board of directors holding just one share each. These numbers demonstrate that Betts had nearly total control over the board, to protect his large investment. One can assume the other members of the board, with their one share each – likely a legal requirement to be a board member – were there to support whatever decisions Betts made.

The business office of the mine shifted locations from Portland to Seattle to Spokane, depending on which corporation was in control. The mine's board of directors met in those cities, met in Mitchell, Oregon (about halfway between the mines and Portland) as well as many early meetings at a location named "Black Butte, Oregon."

Following is an unsolved mystery. Black Butte is a volcanic mountain near Sisters, Oregon. There was no town, so named, near the butte, when the board met. The closest town to Black Butte mountain was, and is, a resort named Camp Sherman (of Civil War name origin), in the Black Butte area. Perhaps the mine board met at Camp Sherman and called it Black Butte.

A resort community called Black Butte was started in that area in 1975. These locations are at least an eight hour drive, on today's highways, from Cornucopia. The exact location of the board meeting site listed so many times as Black Butte in the documents is unverifiable. According to Oregon Geographic Atlas, there is was a tiny town of Black Butte, Oregon, south of Eugene, existing from the 1890's to the 1950's. This locale is too far away from any possible route between Portland and Eastern Oregon, likely geographic criteria for a board meeting site. The mystery location remains unsolved.

The Board of Directors decided to sell the mine in the fall of 1941. Ledgers show record profits between 1939 and 1940. Then, during the period 1940-1941, the mine suddenly lost $77,000. The board voted on September 9th of 1941 for "dissolution and complete liquidation" of the mine and all its assets. This was before Pearl Harbor. One can speculate that the best ore was gone, and the remaining deep ore was too expensive to mine. After Pearl Harbor, by January of 1942, investors were paid individual dividends for stock from a total low of .35 cents to the highest pay-out of $3,236. Some of the surface machinery was sold off for metal scrap during World War Two. During the war, most gold mines were shut down by the government.

After World War Two the mine was maintained as much as a limited budget would allow, gradually falling into disrepair. Taxes mounted, and once again, the mine was bankrupt. According to Howard Brook's outstanding book *A Pictorial History of Gold Mining in the Blue Mountains of Eastern Oregon*, Earl Belle gained control of the mine and properties in 1957. He started issuing and selling Cornucopia Mines stock, keeping the money and apparently not funding any mine development work. He was charged with 31 counts of stock fraud. It is reported that Belle moved to Brazil with about $1,000,000 of mine money.

The mine was bankrupt again in 1958. The mine, its thousand acres, all the remaining buildings and tunnels, sold at a tax-delinquent sale in 1959 for the astoundingly low sum of $11,000. Bust, yet again, but no boom followed. Cornucopia Mine stock was removed by the U.S. Security and Exchange Commission in 1960, according to Brooks.

The business of the mine was run no differently than any other high risk business that survived or sunk against overwhelming odds, weathering a 1908 stock market crash, World War One and the great depression of the 1930s. The mine did not survive World War Two.

United Nuclear is primarily a uranium mining company. Gold mining was a secondary business. United Nuclear appears to be negotiating amounts of mandated court settlement payments as a result of environmental damage lawsuits against them, in regards to mining practices in the

CORNUCOPIA MINES OWNERSHIP RECORD

➤ Oregon Gold Mining Co., based in Louisville Kentucky, starting in 1885, bankrupt in 1895.

➤ Union Company Mines, owned by John E. Searles, bankrupt in 1904.

➤ Cornucopia Mines of Oregon, starting in 1907, bankrupt 1908.

➤ Cornucopia Mines of New York, starting in 1909.

➤ Cornucopia Mines (NY) purchases the Last Chance from Baker Mines Co., Queen of the West Mine and Baker Mill, 1915.

➤ B.B. McGinnis (Canadian) purchased an option to buy Cornucopia Mines, in 1924, invested $15,000 in roads and mill, bankrupt in 1925. Mines idle, very few records for 1925 and 1926.

➤ Cornucopia Mines Company, incorporated in Oregon, operations restarted in 1927. Principal stockholder, Robert Betts.

➤ Cornucopia Gold Mines, incorporated in the State of Washington, starting in 1930. Betts continues management involvement with the mine until his death in the late-1930's.

➤ Earl Belle purchased an option to buy Cornucopia Mines in 1957. Belle bankrupted the mine, fled to South America.

➤ Pittsburg Corporation purchased the mines in 1961.

➤ United Nuclear bought Cornucopia Mines in the late 1970's, lost control of mine to creditor General Electric in the early 1990's.

➤ General Electric Co. obtained mines, apparently, as they were majority financers for United Nuclear. The date is unverified, calls to General Electric not returned.

southwest. One of the largest plaintiff groups in court records against United Nuclear Co. is the Navajo Nation. In the future, court ordered settlements may be a kind of odd indirect form of time-lapse retribution for the original theft of mining lands from Nez Perce and Umatilla tribes. That retribution may not occur to the tribes if attorneys take most of the proceeds. Litigation, like gold mining is risky.

Lode mining is always a volatile business, a real life and death struggle for any gold mining business. Survival is in continuous question, even though Cornucopia Mines processed, during its peak production, 150 *tons* of ore daily, resulting in a gold laden concentrate shipped to the smelter of 2 *tons* per day. Prior to the 1930's depression, economic panic and a small depression occurred in 1907 and 1920. According to the 1981 issue of *Pine Valley Echoes*, Vol. 3, in 1939 the mine profit was 12 cents from each dollar spent on production. During the depression, this was a fair return for a dollar invested, but very risky considering the context of the mining industry. During the depression gold value was advanced from $20 to $35 per ounce via order of FDR.

The lowest year's total in production for lode mining in Oregon was clearly 1929. Statewide 1929 production, from smelter totals, was a total of approximately 5,000 ounces, or just above 300 pounds of gold. Compare that to statewide production totals, in the years of 1903 to 1905 of approximately 60,000 ounces per year, or 3,700 pounds, over ten times the 1929 production total. 1940 was Oregon's top year for gold production. Although placer mining totals produced more gold, companies combined, Cornucopia Mines – individually – still produced far more gold than the top placer (dredging) company in the state, in any given year. Gold production records utilize the current monetary value of gold to calculate profit totals.

The 1905 monetary value total for gold production, for the entire state was $1,300,000. Compare that to a statewide total in 1940, close to $4,000,000. By 1942, the statewide total gold production had plummeted to near zero. The 1942 U.S. legislative ban on mining of non-strategic metals was the primary reason the mine remained closed.

Development and transportation costs were a looming fiscal disaster the mine had to continually fend off. Cornucopia Mines never could afford to fund a railroad access spur line directly to the mine. A major factor affecting mine profit is railroad and smelter proximity, the cost to haul ore to the smelter. Horse-drawn wagons hauled ore shipments, called concentrates, down from Cornucopia Mine to the railhead, as late as the 1920's.[10]

In the old west, as today, an individual gold prospector rarely owns a developed mine. More prevalent are mines or claims being sold by the miner or prospector to a corporation. The development of a mine, including but not limited to mine hoisting and drilling equipment, a rock crushing mill, are all extremely expensive costs. According to recent articles in two separate mine engineering journals, it currently costs between 200 million to a half a billion dollars in total development costs to start up a new gold mine before seeing any profit. Most mines incur very high transportation costs for shipping materials to smelters. Mines did not generally own smelters.

Development is a mining term most often meaning excavation work to reach and work the vein of ore. Development could also mean the cost of the land, also a term to describe setting up surface structures: hoist house, crushers, sorters and even roads. Corporations often paid for the expensive development work through public stock sales. Dishonest corporations involved in the mining industry sold large volumes of stock in worthless or even non-existent mines.

Most stock investors lived on the eastern U.S. seaboard and in England. Apparently there was a prevalent myth in England that one could readily obtain wealth by investing in western mines.

Oregon Governor George Chamberlain first brought attention to this issue in his 1907 "Governor's Regular Session Message." This message is delivered to the legislature every two years. For an item to appear in the Governor's address meant it has special importance and priority for the entire state. Chamberlain's message included:

> Mining is one of the most promising industries in the state, and those engaged in the legitimate work thereof ought to be protected against imposition and impostors ....{a legislative committee should} prepare a bill for the punishment of mining fakers and promoters of illegitimate mining enterprises, and I presume it will be submitted to you. A law has recently been passed by the California Legislature along these lines, and reports are that it has worked an almost complete riddance from that state of spurious mining stock and that lecherous parasite on the mining industry—the fake promoter. The State has been seriously injured by the sale of spurious mining stock throughout the east...any person who undertakes to sell or assent to the publication, privately or publicly, of a fraudulent or exaggerated report tending to give any

person or the public the idea of a greater value than such stock really possesses, with intent to defraud, ought to be deemed guilty of a felony and punished accordingly.[11]

Early 1900's gold mine stock fraud could be compared to the dot.com, the financial industry, the recent real estate and bank failure 'busts.' Since 1907, few mining corporations have been prosecuted by the federal authorities for theft of funds from Oregon stockholders. It was the domain of federal authorities to monitor the situation, but little stock was sold to investors within the state of Oregon. One local example is cited in *Pine Valley Echoes* regarding federal prosecution of owners of local area mines. The nearby Red Ledge and Seven Devils mines were thrown into bankruptcy, after a federal audit in 1927 revealed the owners had perpetrated stock fraud on the stockholders.

It is likely that the laws enacted by Oregon legislation helped stop unethical mine ownership corporations from fleecing local investors. The abuses reported in the Governor's message were perpetrated by large, often phony out of state corporations. Over the years, Cornucopia Mine stayed free of the taint of stock manipulation, with the exception of Earl Belle the pirate. Shareholders received dividends. Cornucopia Mines stock was mainly held by Betts and investors living in Portland and Spokane, Washington, where the headquarters for the corporation was last sited. A majority of mine ownerships have always been in the hands of corporations, which rely on government subsidies to reduce transportation cost. Investors owning Cornucopia Mines expected dividends, and they were paid. It was difficult, during the depression, to raise capital for development projects, especially a risky venture like a gold mine, particularly a mine that had been bankrupt many times.

The closet railroad line to the mine arrived in 1922. The railhead was reached via twenty miles of twisty wagon, then truck road through Pine Creek canyon to the mouth of the Powder River, at the town site of Robinette. The former rail head town site of Robinette was flooded by the Snake River's Brownlee Reservoir in the mid-1950's.[12] Having a closer railroad access at Robinette, sound fiscal management and hard working miners allowed the mine to keep operating through much of the 1920's, when many other mines closed. A map in the Oregon Historical Atlas shows, inaccurately, a spur railroad line extending from Robinette to Baker. On the old map, the railroad line was falsely shown crossing Eagle Creek near the settlement of New Bridge, which was a few miles closer to Cornucopia than the real railhead at Robinette.

During the depression a government funded W.P.A. road building project created a truck-usable road up to the Cornucopia Mine. It was called the 'bootleg grade.' This name was due to a work stoppage by the road builders until enough bootleg whiskey was delivered to satisfy the thirsty crew. It is reported that when the whiskey stopped, work stopped. The road building crew cared nothing about mine stock dividends; but about their whiskey supply.

After the mine mill has done its best at reducing the ore to its lightest possible state, gold ore must be shipped and processed by a smelter. Small amounts of free gold, nuggets or flakes, sometimes naturally separate from the gangue. Gangue means a mix of rock, existing in mines like Cornucopia. Mined ore is crushed, then sorted and chemically refined prior to shipping to a smelter for further refinement into pure gold. Gold is often imbedded inside other rock. Often the mix of rocks containing gold does not have an appearance of gold color. In the Wallowas, hornblende and biotite are common minerals, combined with primary rocks: quartz, granite, schist, hornfels, greywackes, talc and shales. The gold bearing quartz ore was deposited in the cracks of an older, sheared layer of quartz.

A complicated chemical process is necessary to separate the gold from the surrounding minerals and rock. Gold does not want to leave its mineral neighbors; it exists in a subterranean universe of rock, with its own constellations. The floatation milling and final smelting processes precipitate out silver, lead, copper and other minerals that were originally closely mixed in with the gold.

When mines set up floatation and amalgamation process mills near the mine, shipping and smelter costs were greatly reduced. The Cornucopia had a series of mills using various chemical processes. Crushing ore brings it to a size that can be chemically treated. A gravity-based crushing and milling system was utilized by all three Cornucopia Mine mills.

According to Jim Eppling's paper about Cornucopia Mines (Eastern Oregon University Library in La Grande), in 1901 a strike was made that had rich enough ore to allow the company to afford to ship untreated ore directly to a smelter in Tacoma. This is a rare exception to the rule of having to treat ore in a mill near the mine site, reducing the ore weight before shipping to the smelter.

Miners call a mine's entrance tunnel an adit or portal (an outside opening). The collar is the area immediately surrounding the portal. Cornucopia's Union Mine, with both the Union and the Clark adits, had a mill near the Union adit. Later, down the mountain, the Coulter adit had a mill near the mine entrance to process ore. The Baker Mill, also confusingly known as the Cornucopia Mill, and the Union Mill were both dismantled with equipment moved downhill to the Coulter Mill around 1936. Baker Mill was built to process just Queen of the West and Last Chance Mine ore.

A state of the art floatation process mine mill was constructed at the Coulter adit and first processed ore in 1938. There were other early mine mills in the area owned by other mines, mills called the Mayflower and Hoke. Cornucopia mines bought the Last Chance and Queen of the West mines, and their mills, upstream from the town of Cornucopia.

Cornucopia Mines contained 21 distinct connected levels; combining Union, Last Chance and Coulter levels, each level usually engineered 100 feet vertical feet from the next. Not counted is the sump level below level 21. On the mine map it is shown how low the Coulter Tunnel ties into the system – at the 21st level, near the town of Cornucopia.

Cornucopia's thirty-six miles of tunnels were, at various times, worked from three portals or adits: Coulter, Union, and Last Chance. Comparing, for example, the Pentagon's total of 17.5 miles of corridors, thirty-six miles of gold mine tunneling amounts to tremendous development expense. The Last Chance was known as a 'pocket mine' at one time, meaning gold concentrated in small areas of the vein. The Coulter adit is at 4800 feet elevation. At the top of the ridge one shaft surfaced high up on the mountain, engineered well above avalanche danger just to draw fresh air into the entire mine system, at close to 7,500 feet, near Cornucopia Peak. The Union Mine adit is at approximately 5,800 feet. Up the steep mountain is the Last Chance Mine adit, at 6,900 feet.

Stopes, or large areas underground mined upward were given names like: Lawrence, Cop, Wallingford and Valley View (also the names of veins), Bonanza, Snowdrift and Onion Jones. Onion Jones; was it named for a miner's bad breath? The 1930's Coulter adit allowed miners to use miles of chutes carved out between levels; gravity was used to move rock down towards the crushers, rather than haul ore down the mountain by wagons. Even after the Coulter was completed, some ore was still hauled down the mountain from the Union adit by caterpillar tractor and trailer. It is likely that this method was used when the ore body was close to the surface adit.

Two miles of steep mountainside separate the highest and the lowest adits. The cross section map of the mine shows a view of all the levels of the mine. The road from Coulter adit up to the Union adit is notched against precipitous cliffs in places. According to miner interviews, the rough four wheel drive road one takes today, while walking or horseback riding up to the Union adit, is improved from the road of the 1930's.

The road up to Union and Last Chance adits was built at considerable expense. There are few level areas on the mountain between adits. Three of the levels of the Cornucopia Mines complex had direct horizontal access, with mine car tracks to the outside. When the adits were first blasted in, the waste rock from the excavation provided a level surface that served as a staging area to position mining equipment and materials like timbering. Mining engineers, fighting the random structure of minerals underground, create as-efficient-as-possible ore movement systems.

Inside the mine, upon occasion there is a chiaroscuro of color in the rock: grey, red, white, brown, beige, black, and once in a while bits of gold. To get the ore out at the least possible cost, the mine carved ore chutes between levels. They were lined by smooth timbers, so rock did not get hung up on its way down, and clog the chute. Each level had a heavy wooden chute stop-gate at the bottom. There was a specified amount of ore that filled the chute from higher levels, so ore would not become so heavy from above that a miner at a lower level could not open the chute. Chutes were opened to fill each ore car, then closed while the next ore car was brought forward. Once filled, the entire train of cars took the ore out the adit to the sorting house in the mill.

Next to ore chutes was space for ladders, partitioned off from the chute. The ladders were used so miners could climb or descend from one level to the other to maintain the chutes, or for exit in case of emergency. Metal skips, like crude elevators, carried miners up and down Cornucopia's inclined main shaft went from level 6 to level 13. Miners would ride into the mine in small ore cars, sometimes riding on the same cars that were carrying the timbering material into the mine. Then, the miner would get in a skip and be lowered or raised to the work area.

Mine engineers followed the most productive veins. The veins were a mixture of waste rock, gold, silver, lead and copper minerals. The veins themselves had names: Union-Companion, Last Chance, the smaller Wallingford and Valley View. These veins lie along the southwestern edge of what's called the Cornucopia Stock – a small offshoot of the gigantic Wallowa Mountains Batholith formation.[13]

Ore hauled to the mill comes mixed with some worthless rock to be discarded through hand sorting. Once sorted to remove waste rock from the mix, ore is crushed by a ball mill or stamp mill. The less ore that is crushed, the less expense: thus the necessity of hand sorting ore at an early stage in the process. A ball mill utilized rotating ore bins containing hundreds of metal or rock balls, about the size of small baseballs, mixed with the ore as the bin rotated. A stamp mill utilized a battery of stamps, mounted pistons in a row, so incoming ore is smashed as it passed under the stamps, vertically from above.

Early 1900's Cornucopia milling methods consisted of: sorting and crushing, then below the crushing area were ore bins, below the bins, a large room containing a long row of concentrating tables called vanners. Vanners were also known as settling tables. The entire vanner operation was called a concentrator line. A vanner table shook and at the same time held in grooves the finer sized ore, combining it with mercury or cyanide.

The result of this industrial process was an impure amalgamation of gold, a bit of fine sand, other metals, and the mercury or cyanide not washed out in the processing system. The economic panic of 1907 and bankruptcy of Cornucopia Mines stopped all development work at the mine. By 1912, there was a new owner and new capitol to convert the mill at the Union Portal into a slime-Cyanide plant. The resulting mix of this process was shipped in bags to the smelter for refining. Less shipping weight and lower smelter costs were two of the results of the new process. The final product of the mills was a mixture of gold, minerals and chemicals, dried in furnaces to reduce shipping costs, a concentrate ready for shipping to the smelter to remove all impurities and perform a final separation of the minerals within the concentrate. A complicated series of chemical processes at the smelter, usually involving heat and cyanide, resulted in bars or a conical shaped ingot called a dore, which was nearly pure gold.

The closet ore smelting works to Cornucopia was in the town of Sumpter, some 85 miles distant. No records can be located of Cornucopia ore ever being processed by the Sumpter smelter. The Sumpter smelter operated, on and off, from 1904 to the early 1930's. It shut down during much of the 1920's due to a low volume of ore available. After the Sumpter smelter burned down, including its records, Cornucopia ore, if it was ever shipped to Sumpter, had to be shipped to distant smelters.

What else can be imagined as a fate for a smelter, where hot ore reduction brick furnaces burn inside wooden buildings? The steam power furnaces providing the smelter with electricity also fired in a ramshackle wooden mill complex. Smelting plants had a very high fire risk. Two gigantic gold ore smelters burned down in the Cripple Creek Colorado area. Over the years, where the ore was routed depended on the rates the smelters charged combined with transportation costs. By the 1930's the nearest smelters to isolated Cornucopia were in Tacoma, Washington, East Helena, Montana, and the San Francisco Bay Area. These cities had ample infrastructure to support smelters.

Electricity and telephone were both slow to arrive at Cornucopia town and mine. Telephone lines did not arrive at the mine until the 1920s. Electricity, enough for the mine buildings, was generated by the mines hydro-electric system on Pine Creek. About two miles below the Coulter Tunnel was a power house containing generating turbines. Just below the town, part of Pine Creek was diverted into a ditch running nearly level. The water was then run down hill in a sharp drop, where it entered and turned the generating turbines. The main problem with this power system was low creek flow during summers.

During times of low stream flow, wood fired power generators were used. Due to the expense to install power generators and lines, the mines were not fully electrified until 1922. The Union Mine first used electrical power, according to *Pine Valley Echoes*, Vol. 1, when the electrical generating plant was built down on Pine Creek in 1900. An additional electric generating plant was built on upper Pine Creek in 1915. With more electricity generating power a new, larger 20 stamp mill was installed at the mine, resulting in recovery of a larger percentage of gold from the ore.

In 1920 the Cornucopia owned Last Chance mine buildings burned down. Once again fiscal disaster loomed. For the next decade the Baker Mill, thousands of feet down the valley, was idle. Apparently, it was not economically feasible to move Last Chance ore on existing roads to the Union Mine mill. The two mines were not yet connected underground. Yet in 1920, a time of economic recession, the mine owners opted to keep their miners working to run an expensive new shaft to link up the lower workings of their Last Chance Mine with upper levels of their Union Mine. According to a 4/08/1920 article in the *New York Times*:

> New York stockholders of the Washington Power Co. are {also} stockholders of the Cornucopia Co. There are not many gold properties that can be mined at the present time, so the company is confining most of its work to this development. Cornucopia proper will not be worked until gold conditions {price} improve..."

Fiscal problems, possible failure, were always present. One of the largest public bond failures in the history of our nation was the failure of the Washington State Public Power System, known by the public as 'whoops.' Even though his massive fiscal failure came much later in the 20th century, it is ironic that record show that Cornucopia stockholders, when the company was based in Seattle, invested in not one, but two very risky organizations; the mine and WSPPS, 'whoops.'

Cornucopia's Baker Mill restarted in 1930, milling the existing surface tailing piles from Last Chance and Queen of the West. This was fiscally sound when the chemical processing method improved to allow the mill to extract gold at well above the cost of reprocessing the ore. There were no mining costs incurred, obviously, with this method. Some cables from the old Last Chance and Queen of the West Mine tramways were recycled into a system to haul buckets of ore back into the mill from the tailing piles.

Jared Herdlick, an interview with his wife follows, was instrumental in engineering the restart of Cornucopia's Baker Mill. This was followed by the construction of a newer mill at the Coulter adit. According to mine records, in both cases machinery was recycled from local mills and used machinery was purchased from defunct mines in Arizona, California and Utah.

The 1937 electrified stamp mill, near the Coulter adit, crushed sixty tons of ore a day. Gold processing in 1910 recovered about 65 percent of available gold from the raw ore. Switching from mercury to a new heated cyanide process, in 1937, 90 percent of the gold was recovered from ore. Quoted in *Pine Valley Echoes, Vol 3*:

> The ore...was exceptionally rich going between $16 and $18 per ton. The rock milled was high grade pet-site which is found in only two other places in the world, one of these being Cripple Creek, Colorado.

When the Coulter adit opened, ore could be carted directly from the mine portal to the newer ball crushing facility nearby, then by gravity to the nearby floatation cyanide process building. This replaced the older vanner table process used up the mountain at the demolished Union mill. Finely crushed ore was mixed with cyanide and other chemicals in large metal tanks. The tanks were heated. There were large mixing wheels inside each tank to stir the ore slurry. The new Coulter adit mill was state-of-the-art. Ore crushing was now made more efficient by use of a ball mill in addition to use of the older 20 stamp mill. According to a U.S. Forest Service document, available at the Halfway Museum, interviewer Don Mackinson asked a miner named John about the new milling process at the Coulter mill:

> In the mid 30's, they {Cornucopia Mines} could get three or four dollars a ton turning it through the floatation, much more efficient. There's still gold in it...{about the Baker mill tailings} They had three dump trucks run around the clock, winter and summer. They didn't have to blade the road or nothing, they just kept it packed.

The new cyanide processing system was clearly a health hazard to the mill workers. Gold mining and milling is both dangerous and toxic work. Jobs like scuba diving in caves and underwater welding come to mind. Small mistakes can easily bring death. One is working, after all, with toxic chemicals, and dynamite, in very confined spaces.

The most dangerous of all the tasks of a gold miner would be removing unexploded dynamite from a recently blasted surface, inside a rock face, amongst the rubble resulting from the other sticks explosions. Cornucopia gold miner Dale Holcomb later describes the disastrous results of one such incident. Gold miners' jobs involved improvising tasks, in semi-darkness, at the edge of death.

Doctors were hired by the mine or paid a retainer for piece work.

There is a large white house on Main Street in Halfway, by the old telephone office, built by the company for Dr. Pollock. Also treating Cornucopia gold miners over the years, according to *Pine Valley Echoes* magazine, were Doctors: Strange, Walsh, Sanders, O'Conner, Estabrook and Dr. Williams serving as a part time dentist.

At peak employment in the early 1900's the mine; mill and all other operations employed over 700 people. By 1930 Cornucopia Gold Mines Co. had acquired all the major mines in the area. Automation and efficiency reduced the workforce to 300, still a huge workforce in a remote area with few other jobs. Even during the depression, the mine hired new employees on a regular basis, replacing those who were injured, fired or retired. There was an occasional market driven layoff, making gold miners very concerned about the stability of their jobs.

Cornucopia miner, machinist and caretaker Chris Schneider states empathetically (quote from *Pine Valley Echoes* magazine):

> In 1937 they laid off 30 men....some of them were hit hard. I feel sorry for them.

Cornucopia Gold Miners never had union representation. As both miner Dale and superintendent's spouse Bonnie explain in subsequent pages, the company paid well and treated their workers with care. Jobs were scarce enough to negate the possibility of a union being voted in by the workers. Miner's union activity was rare in Eastern Oregon. There is evidence of local union activity. The author has an original 1906 charter for the "Central Labor Union" of Baker, signed by American Federation of Labor national President Samuel Gompers. One gold miner name is listed as an officer. There is some additional evidence of local union activity, a few historic photos of a mine union organizer giving a speech, in the Baker Library archives.

Famous United Mine Workers' Union leaders such as John L. Lewis primarily supported the rights of coal miners in the Eastern part of the United States. Miner's unions often struggle to force owners to implement life saving safety methods and equipment. There was the infamous, allegedly corrupt, United Mine Workers' Union leader Tony Boyle of the 1960's. The miner's union has a large scale mine focus. Baker area mines are small in scale. This factor seems to have curtailed union membership. Certainly mine ownership, operating on a thin profit margin, struggling to survive, did not want union activity. The senior miners apparently were not interested, either, in union membership. They were interested in helping out the younger miners safely learn their trade, and learn their mines, and stay alive. Gold miners, like many of the residents of Baker County, lean towards the conservative side of the political scale.

Nevertheless, Baker County voted for Franklin D. Roosevelt in all his presidential contests. Baker County's pro-Roosevelt voter percentages varied from 51 percent to 63 percent during his four elections.[14] These FDR presidential Oregon victories include the 1940 race, when Oregon Senator Charles McNary was the Republican Vice-Presidential candidate. Apparently, this local connection did not strongly influence miners' voting. It is possible that if one interviewed 20 Oregon miners one would obtain 20 different political opinions. It seems the local miners' politics were on the micro-level of kindness towards their brother miners.

New miners occasionally become lost in the vast tunnel system. It was a Cornucopia Mines procedure, due to the complexity of the tunnel system, to require new workers to always go underground with veteran miners. The largest shafts run out to the levels of the portals, a bit like underground highways. Stopes were often connected vertically by the ladders or at least to a level that has horizontal access to a mechanical lift. Moving to and from the ore face took expensive, paid time. Getting lost was inefficient and dangerous. A miner's unpaid winter commute to work to the mine adit from their cabin to work sometimes took more than an hour, one way. In the early 1900's the daily work hours were long. According to a Pearl Jones article in the April 24, 2006 *Baker City Herald*, gold miner Harry J. Belden stated:

> We worked 12 hours a day, 11 hours on Saturday and 10 hours on Sunday. That was called short shift. While I was there...they changed from 12 to 10 hour shifts. We had so much time in the evening, we didn't know what to do. I was there about three months when they changed foremen again and we all got fired. So went my initiation into life as a miner...they had taken out a candle box full of ore and there was $11,000 worth of gold in it.

The miners worked hard during extended hours for what would be now considered low wages. Yet, they believed they were well paid, considering the economic conditions. Muckers, shoveling waste rock and ore all day into ore cars, had incredibly demanding physical jobs. Cornucopia Mines went to considerable expense to make miners dangerous lives easier.

One mile inside the Coulter tunnel, in the mid 1930's, the company blasted out a dining room space inside an empty stope of the mine. One can imagine the conditions in the underground dining room. An even floor of rock would have been a priority. This was a very basic tables-and benches lunch room full of banter and jokes. It is recorded that the company cook fed the miners large and tasty meals. There was a modest fee for the meals. The inside-the-mine dining room allowed the miners to spend more time working underground, and less break time going to and from the surface cookhouse for lunch. Sadly, no photos are known to exist of the underground dining room.

There are photos inside the mine's mess hall, outside the Union adit. There is a restaurant look to the dining room: china, table cloths, bowls of fruit, even wine glasses are visible in the photo. This photo may have recorded a special holiday meal.

Why does a meal at a ski resort cost an outrageous amount of money? Resort food is brought into a remote mountain location and sold at a very high price to a captive audience with no alternatives. Clearly, the mine made costly efforts to provide the miners with a quality food as a very reasonable price, despite the fact that the mine could have charged hungry miners 'ski resort' prices for their meals.

According to *Pine Valley Echoes* magazine, in the 1930's the company built three rows of houses in Cornucopia which included electricity and plumbing, some with a second story for mine officers' families. Two sources indicate that the rent was reasonable. When the mine closed, some of those company houses were later moved down the valley to Halfway, where they may be currently identified by their small size and steep roof pitches. One would easily bump one's head in the limited headroom upper bedrooms.

In the early 1930's the company implemented and enforced a rule that each miner must wear a hard hat at all times. This rule was resisted by the miners, mainly because they had to buy the hard hats. Ear protection from excessive noise was unheard of. Power equipment rooms roared with noise inside the mine. Precious underground space was carved out to house large water pumps and hoisting engines. It was a huge expense to the company to haul high cost industrial equipment up the mountain and inside the mine. Assembling, installing and maintaining such intricate machinery, underground in the wet environment increases the expense.

The company continually recycled equipment, whenever possible, from their own mines. Equipment needs replacement at the same time production must be maintained. In the mills, ore processing methods changed so new equipment was often needed above ground. The high cost of upgrading equipment constantly raised the question of the fiscal survival of the mine.

Supervisors, engineers, surveyors, industrial planners, map makers and other workers all fulfilled vital functions that directly influenced profitability. Excavating longer, wider or higher than necessary tunnels incurred unneeded expense and was avoided. The company's survival depended on getting the ore out as cheaply and quickly as possible. Gold is a global market. In other nations, miners work for lower wages. The brutal fact that the vast majority of gold mines in United States become bankrupt surely kept the management team at Cornucopia Mines vigilant. It took all the mine work teams working in efficient sequence to make Cornucopia Mines profitable. The teams were paid at different wage levels, both underground and surface.

Union Mine wages in 1898 averaged $3.50 per day, for a 12 hour day. Amazingly, during the next 40 years, miner wages increased slightly less than one dollar per day. The daily hours of required work decreased. There were two economic depressions during those same 40 years. The author's collection includes over 800 Cornucopia Mines worker timecards, written by mine supervisors during the period 1937 to 1940. The average pay of miners and millworkers was 63 cents per hour. Timecards reveal the following job titles and wages in cents per hour:

Miner	72	Mucker	60
Operator	71	Drilling	56
Hoistman	66	Motor Helper	66
Timberman	66	Track Layer	53
Nipper	66	Assayer (mill)	75
Truck Helper	66	Electrician	60
Watchman	38	Tramming	66

The highest paid non-management worker in the mine, according to the 1930's timecards, was bulldozer operator Walt Bishop. Walt had the dangerous job of keeping the snow cleared from the steep road up to the Union adit, and keeping the road maintained during summer. At other times, Walt worked as a lower wage trammer man hauling ore or waste out or materials or supplies into the mine.

Using an average wage, a 1939 Cornucopia worker would realize $4.40 a day for a six day work week totaling a weekly wage of $26.40. This weekly pay roughly coincided with the cost of a set of work clothing. Miners needed to buy two sets of work clothing. Due to the wet conditions in the mine, one set of clothes was left at the end of the shift in the drying room. That way, the miners would always have a dry set of clothes to get into at the beginning of the next shift. A minor purchased, usually through the company store, items which were deducted from his pay. A 1919 Cornucopia Mines recruiting letter, targeting returning World War One veterans, indicated that the mine would provide rain pants and coats for free. Following is a typical set of clothes and boots needed for work. The amounts are recorded on late 1930's mine purchase records:

Short boots	$3.75	Rubber pants	$3.65
Gloves 4 pair	$1.17	Hat	$3.26
Hip boots	$4.60	Rain coat	$4.20
Sweat shirt	.65c	Belt	.80c
Coat	$2.25	Union suit	$2.00

Total clothing cost, one set = $29.08

Names on miners' time cards from the 1930's reveal different national origins. Cornish miners called 'Cousin-Jacks,' Nordic, Italian, German and possibly Native American names also emerge from the timecards. The Cornish enjoyed purchasing 'fancy' formal clothing in Baker City, used during Cornucopia holiday dances on Labor Day and Christmas. Imagine the fun; Cornish miners dressed in swallowtail coats and their ladies in hoop skirts, and roughly dressed miners and calico dress women spinning reels at the dance hall, as Chris Schneider's family band jammed away. Some miners had families living with them in the towns of Cornucopia or Halfway. A gold miner supporting a large family was obviously motivated by a need for a steady source of income.

Notwithstanding wage issues, the lust for gold is a powerful motivator. Workers take dangerous jobs in mines because it is a job in a remote area having few other jobs. Some work in the mines, in part, due to a gambling tendency within themselves. Even as a base level miner, there is always the possibility of a bonus, beyond wages, from an employer who reaps windfall profits. Miners and owners alike always hope to strike it rich.

In the earlier days of the mine, when the ore was of a higher grade, a few Cornucopia miners stole ore, a practice called 'high grading.' Bonanza level gold strikes are uncovered upon rare occasions. Gold mines in other states have produced immense, fabulous wealth. Unlike Cornucopia, some wealthy Colorado gold mines had close access to railroads and smelters. Cornucopia miners certainly heard of a mine phenomenon called the Cresson vug. The Cresson Mine and the Cornucopia Mine deserve comparison.

The Cornucopia, by far the richest in Oregon, compares with the Cresson. If you combine the current placer earnings at the huge Cresson with the historic Cresson lode earnings, it is likely the richest gold mine in Colorado. There were other contending mines for highest gold production in Colorado. The Cresson, near Cripple Creek Colorado, operates today as an open pit mine.

In 1914, a small crew of miners 800 feet down in the Cresson Mine broke through the stope wall into an exceptionally rare mine vug. The richest gold bearing vug ever found. A vug is caused by ancient geologic-volcanic forces, creating a large bubble like cave in the earth. Sometimes vugs contain no valuable rock. Think of a giant bubble, a geode inside the earth, the hollow type with crystals inside a void in the geode. A huge thunder egg. The Cresson vug was the fulfillment of miner's pirate treasure dreams. The Cresson vug measured 40 feet high by 15 feet wide and 20 feet long. The walls, floor and ceiling solidly glistened with pure flakes of gold, mostly thumbnail sized, slightly mixed with quartz. What a sight the vug must have been. One black and white photograph of the underground room full of gold was taken, and survives on a postcard. Color photography didn't exist at the time, a drawing of the vug also appeared in a magazine.

Cresson Mine manager Richard Roeloff immediately ordered a steel door installed inside the mine, at the vug entrance, bolted and riveted in. Armed guards were posted at the vug doors, day and night. When the Cresson vug was mined out, it yielded a 2006 dollar value close to $20 million, the vug alone. In 1914 dollars, the vug brought the mine owners nearly $1,200,000.[15]

The Cresson vug glittered miraculously, dazzling miners with an almost religious awe. Mother Nature revealed one of her most secret and precious treasures to the Cresson miners. It took nearly four weeks to mine the gold off the walls, floor and ceiling of the vug. The rich ore was sent under armed guard to the smelter for a final refinement. A false rumor flew amongst the miners of the nation that some of the Cresson Vug gold was shipped directly to the U.S. mint for coin manufacture. All Cresson Vug ore was taken by guarded wagons two miles down to the railhead. From there the ore was taken to the smelter in Colorado Springs.

Due to profits from the vug, Cresson built an extensive aerial tramway, one of the highest elevation mine tramway in the United States. The Queen of The West Mine tramway (eventually owned by Cornucopia Mines) was at a similar elevation. The Cresson tramway bucketed processed mine ore two or three miles down Eclipse Gulch directly to the railroad siding. Machinery was upgraded. Stock holders and managers received large dividends and miners received hefty bonuses. The formerly frugal mine manager Richard Roeloff eventually retired to a mansion in New York City. The underground Cresson Mine would go on producing until 1961, when the nearby smelter closed down, making ore transportation cost prohibitively expensive, even for a mine as rich as the Cresson.

Extensive gold ore still exists underground at the Cresson, similar to Cornucopia's situation. Cresson Mine resumed production in 2001. The surrounding mountains were surface excavated in gigantic steps, reaching down to the upper levels of the original workings of the historic Cresson lode mine. Mine company earth moving machinery was preceded by use of ground penetrating radar to identify places where machinery might fall into the historic mine stopes. At the vug of the Cresson, lucky miners broke into the golden heart of the mountain, an auriferous mineral structure of priceless breathtaking beauty.

Cornucopia Mines contained no vugs, although high grade veins and pockets of ore were discovered. Cornucopia's Cresson like aerial tramway carried ore from the upper adits on the mountain, down to the Baker mill, above the town. Another Colorado-Cornucopia connection was the name of one of the levels in Cornucopia's Last Chance Mine, called the 'Tabor Level.' This name referred to famous Colorado mine owner and one time Colorado Senator H.A.W. Tabor. Several mine owners, like Tabor, have become government mining officials. One of the original mining claims that were all eventually owned by Cornucopia Mines was named "Senator Tabor." These names indicate somewhat of a blending between private industry and government.

Government policy and regulations, more so today, affect miner's personal safety directly. The 2006 President Bush appointment for Federal Director of Mine Safety was a former mine owner, who likely had mine owners as a priority, not miner safety.

United States government rules stopped the possible reopening the Cornucopia Mine and shut down all other exclusively gold mines with executive order L-208, implemented in early1942.[16] The act was meant to reserve mining resources for metals critical to the war effort, and make more labor available for war time industries. The Cresson of Colorado was one of the few mines allowed to continue production during the war due to other strategic metals needed for the war effort being present in the mine. That law didn't preclude the Cresson from also mining gold during World War Two. They had it both ways.

Eventually, World War Two proved to be a major factor affecting the restarting of production at Oregon's greatest mine. The explosions of Japanese bombs at Pearl Harbor seem to have reverberated across the Pacific into the Cornucopia. After the war: inflation, labor costs, the ravages of time on equipment, rotted timbers, flooded tunnels and cave-ins all combined to make it too expensive to restart production. Yet Cornucopia's buried riches continue to beckon investors. Since the closure, new owners have made expensive developmental explorations in the mine to determine if it was feasible to restart production.

By the late 1970's the Arizona company United Nuclear gained control of the mine. They poured development money into the mine as the price of gold reached $800 per ounce. Compare this to 1884 when gold was $20 per ounce, and 1941, when gold had increased to just $35 per ounce. As of this writing, the price of gold is above $1,000. An ounce, and unlike the sharp spike up and immediate drop in 1980, seems to be staying at that high level for the time being.

Due to the rise in gold prices in the 1970's, the Coulter was reopened and re-timbered. The 1930's Coulter adit had caved, so a new side cut adit was made into the mountain, intersecting the Coulter about 100 yards in. A large new processing mill has been built next to the foundations of the old mill, and some mine mill machinery has been installed. An older ore transfer or sorting house was reinforced and restored near the adit. The 1930's dynamite room appears usable, as it is made of cement walls and ceilings. The 1970's to early 1980's development work determined that ample ore existed in the deeper parts of the mine. This area is private property.

Up the mountain, the 1880's vintage Union adit tunnel house (a long shed covering the tracks, now collapsed by snow) was rebuilt, and a small new tool room was built. The old mine was stirring to life. The town of Cornucopia, by then, was a true ghost town with no existing businesses, just vacation cabins. That ghost was now coming to life. When development money dried up in the early 1980's, the adit, the Coulter tunnel was blasted shut to keep trespassers out.

With the price of gold crashing, United Nuclear suddenly stopped all work at Cornucopia. Within about three months, gold had risen from $400 to over $800, then down to as low as $250 per ounce. The 1980 highest gold price, adjusted for inflation, in 2012 dollars, would be valued at over $2,000 an ounce.

The large new Cornucopia mine mill, a descendant of the vanished Union, Baker and Coulter mills, remains unfinished inside. As of the writing of this book, the current owners of the mine, General Electric, have determined that it is not economically feasible to reopen the mine. G.E. has offered the mine and land for sale. There are over 1,000 acres of beautiful, forested mountain land that are included with the patented mine claims, surrounded by the Wallowa Whitman National Forest and the Eagle Cap Wilderness. Who knows if the mine will ever reopen?

---

[8] Source from: http://halfwayor.com/museum/.

[9] *A Pictorial History of Gold Mining in the Blue Mountains*, Howard Brooks, Baker County Historical Society, 2007, pages 153-159.

[10] *Oregon's Golden Years*, Miles F. Potter, Caxton Printers, Caldwell Idaho, 1976, pages 156-157.

[11] State of Oregon record of Governor George E. Chamberlain, Regular Session Message, Salem, Oregon, State Printer, 1906.

[12] *Oregon's Golden Years*, Miles F. Potter, 1976, page 152.

[13] *Gold Mining in Oregon*, Bert Webber, 1995, page 89.

[14] Loy, William G., Stuart Allan, Aileen R. Buckley and James E. Meacham, *Atlas of Oregon*. Second Edition, Eugene: University of Oregon Press, 2001, page 37.

[15] *Money Mountain*, Marshall Sprague, University of Nebraska Press 1953, pages 274-275.
[16] *Ghost Towns of the Pacific Frontier*, Lambert Florin, 1970, pages 36-38.

CHAPTER 4
MINER AND FAMILY INTERVIEWS

Gotta get down to the Cumberland Mine...That's where I mainly spend my time...Make good money five dollars a day... Make a little more, might move away...heh heh.

"Cumberland Blues" (Garcia, Hunter)[17]

ORAL HISTORY IS AN INTANGIBLE BUT VITAL CULTURAL RESOURCE. Stories, attitudes and values all belong in the domain of cultural history. Physiographic context; mountains, valleys, and creeks all help humans form culture. The gold miners interviewed all have high grade ore inside them, mixed with rocky gravel to form the unique amalgam of their personalities. The Cornucopia area miners and ranchers are rightly proud of the years of hard work developing the mine, the town, and the county. Following are author interviews and a profile of Chris Schneider based primarily on articles in *Pine Valley Echoes*.

Interview with Cornucopia Gold Miner Dale Holcomb
(by the author, at Dale's home, 09/2/2006)

The following comments are used with Dale's permission, mostly made in response to questions by the author at Dale's Victorian farm house outside of Richland, Oregon, about 20 miles south of Cornucopia. Some of the quotes are from later correspondence between Dale and the author. Dale is a virtual gold mine of information. Dale (like Bonnie, interview following) does not at all look like a person in their

90's. One would guess that Dale is 75 to 80 years. He is a very fit and articulate gentleman-farmer, kind and fun to talk with. Dale was born on a farm near Eagle Creek, west of Pine Creek, perhaps 15 miles as the crow flies from Cornucopia Mine. Dale states:

I started out at Cornucopia mines in 1937 as a mucker, then promoted to the drill crew, then as a miner, working in the mine for the contractor Claude Laughten. Us contractors, in a way, worked for American Diamond Drill Company, who supplied us with our drills, bits, etc. Claude hired people, using the equipment leased from American Diamond Drill.

The early mine operators took out only the best ore. We mined the leftovers. Because of the new Cyanide process, we could make money on it.

The Cornucopia mine was a wet mine. They ran pumps all the time to dewater the mine. Walt Blacker filed a claim for the water rights of the part of Pine Creek that ran right out of the Coulter adit. Smart move, he was a rancher.

We wore black long handled union suits, wool socks, canvas pants called 'tin pants,' high laced boots, rubber pants and a slicker. Nobody wore gloves. There weren't any dust masks. You couldn't handle machinery well wearing gloves. We had a drying room that had a big woodstove in the middle, and hooks that went up into the upper part of the room so your clothes would be put up to dry between shifts.

A diamond driller holds his hand under the hole, feeling the findings {materials coming out of the drill hole}. He says, when the drill reaches the vein, 'We're grinding grit.' They pull the core {a narrow cylinder of rock} out of the hole and send it to the assay office for assessment.

Ed Burns, {miner} he would see when there were new guys on the shift. He'd wait till they were looking at him, pull a couple of sticks of dynamite out of his long johns and throw 'em right into the woodstove {in the changing room}. They would run away so fast. Then, there was a big old grin on his face. The dynamite, with no blasting caps, would just burn up like cellophane.

Going in from the Union adit, we went in about 2,500 feet and got in a skip box to be lowered down towards the Coulter shaft. One time, a whole box of dynamite came loose and went rolling down the skip way {inclined shaft}, went all the way down to the next level. It didn't blow up, but you should of seen people scatter when the box rolled bounced next to 'em. Those skips held one ton each.

At the face {inside the mine}, the Craigbaum brothers had drilled and filled the holes with dynamite changes, they cleared out {down the tunnel}. One brother, Kermit, was my friend. The miner who set the charges puts his head right against the wall of the shaft {a safe distance from the blast site} and counts the number {of blasts} he hears {of the dynamite charges just placed and fired in holes at the face}. For safety, you wait up to eight hours; if one of the shots doesn't go off, to go in and to dig it {unexploded dynamite} out by hand. This is extremely dangerous. They went back in, later, and the shot went off in their faces as they were digging it out. Both were blinded, one recovered. To get out without falling down another shaft, they grabbed ahold of the mine cart and pushed it out, staggering, following the car all the way out to the dump stop, {outside the mine}....We did have workers' comp. insurance.

On the main level of the Union mine, the right drift was called the Copenhagen Stope. It was an ungodly big stope, {mined out area} at a 60% pitch, All the pillars {ore left in the older sections of the mine, to support the levels above} had to be hand mined. It was a forest of stulls {timbers}.

The skip {a large metal container, somewhat like an elevator cage, running vertically or at an incline inside the mine} was run by an air hoist. The exhaust froze all the time. The operator had a chisel he kept chipping the ice out of the exhaust. The cars on the skip were narrow and long. Two men could lay on their backs per car. A bellwire ran above the track. You could always contact the operator. Two jerks meant down. Three up. Five {meant} hurry. So, 3 and 5 meant 'up' in a 'hurry.' I forget what stop was. Only material and men were carried {in the skip} No ore.

There was a new guy, just hired, who had heard about some cougars people were shooting near the mine. He asked Claude what to do if he sees a cougar in the mine? Claude says: 'Grab him by the tail, wrap it around a stull, (post) start yelling. We'll come around and knock it with drills.' The new guy quit.

The bosses were real nice guys. The foremen were working foremen, worked right alongside you. Davis and Goodspeed were in charge of everybody. Davis was a helluva operator, so was Goodspeed. The miners all worked well together, no problems there. Miners were paid about $100 a month, very good wages. The bosses also got a percentage of the contractor's ore. There was a company doctor named Pollock, no ambulance, though. The injured were driven out to Baker in private cars. I had a perfect safety record as a miner. Consumption, lungs, killed a lot of them {miners}.

Mainly for safety reasons, you could get fired on the spot. For example, if {one was} caught running a drill, {but had been} hired as a mucker, they're gone. There were 2 or 3 people fired each month, mostly safety violations. In the late 1930's, the mine started making us buy and wear hard hats, we almost went out on strike about that. But, generally, we all worked as a team. There was some resentment about cat skinners {caterpillar operators}'cause they got $1.00 more per hour than the miners. During the depression, it was considered very good pay, top pay. There were no jobs in our corner of Oregon, with those good wages a gold miner could do things like buy a new car.

Each work team had 2 miners, and 2 swampers and 2 muckers . The muckers did stuff like dig, fill the mine cars with both waste and ore, the swampers got the drills and hoses, both helped the miners in any way they could. One time I was working as a mucker, underground in a very narrow space. I was working the 'underhand,' a part of the mine called that, with the Derrick kids. Children of old 'peg leg' Derrick. We hit a pocket of high grade ore, gold mixed with Appelite. I went and got the boss right away. He was pleased, said 'if you was a miner, you'd of carried that out in your lunch box...' Claude told me to go get a sacker at the station, 200 yards away. He stayed with the high grade, then me and him sacked it and took it out. I was promoted from mucker to miner for telling the truth. Claude won his own money, earlier, on the gambling that goes on about the exact minute when the ice breaks up in Fairbanks. He took most of the money and sunk it {lost it} in the Anna mine.

I didn't see any free ore, no free gold. It was base ore. There was gold-looking beautiful ore, but it was other metals like pyrite. No vugs in the mine. There were pockets of higher grade ore, from a few pounds to a couple of tons. I don't know of anyone who high-graded {stole ore}. I suppose there were fences in Baker for gold.

Ed Hensley found a rich pocket of {surface} ore near the Cornucopia. Must have been 3 or 4 feet square. He {picked it loose and} rolled it away and hid it near a cold spring. Ed died, and no-one ever found it.

We all had miner's union cards, had a miner's union, but it was a safety organization only, not a wage bargaining unit. The miner's cards cost from $2.00 to $5.00 a month. That got you in free to the dances, which were 2 or 3 dollars without the card. It was a good deal to get cards. There was a miner's union hall in Cornucopia with monthly dances. Fights were often between miners and cowboys. They all fought a lot. I was in both camps, raising horses at the time and mining.

During one fight, a mine mill worker named Art Moore, he used a cane because he'd been shot in the leg. Art raised his cane to wallop Jim on the head. I was right there, grabbed Art's cane out of his hand, it was heavy, would of knocked Jim clean out. All hell was breaking loose, I went to the corner with the cane. The corner of the union hall had braces to keep the snow from knocking the building in, so I climbed up on a brace with the cane as a weapon. During that brawl, no one bothered me. All they {miners} really cared about was women and booze.

There were some prostitutes in town. At one of the dances, Alex, who liked them, was putting it to her on the front porch. Some guy noticed Alex, pointed out the window towards the porch and started yelling "fight...fight." Some women, that were closest to the door, got pushed out there by the crowd pushing to see the fight. Alex kept at it, at first, then everybody was trying to push out to the porch. The poor women wanted to get away, but the crowds kept 'em there.

It was amazing, the next day people that had been fighting would patch up their differences and go back to work together. The only violence in the mine I ever heard about was some guy named Tucker stabbed another miner with a candlestick way back in the 1920's.

Fred, he was a big guy, a moonshiner in Eagle Valley. I think he lived in Cove near the Snake River. When prohibition ended, he went to work for the mine in the lumber shed cutting wedges. We used a lot of wedges to keep the mine timbers tight. Fred was cutting wedges on a table saw, and a pile behind him fell into him. Knocked him right into the saw, spilt his head down the middle in two pieces. Jimmy bootlegged and peddled his stuff in town {Cornucopia}. He owned the pool hall. A lot of the miners were gamblers. More bootleggers: Clyde, and Herb, over in Eagle Valley.

In Cornucopia, Hayman Swisher owned the best hotel, his bar served visitors, not many miners. At our{miners}bar, beer was .25 cents a bucket, about a quart. It was 3.2 % beer, though.{at this point Dale strides briskly over the cut lawn over to a table on the back porch of his ranch house and grabs an antique beer bucket, complete with original color brand name and filigree design, holding it up with one hand, grinning and pointing at it with the other, saying}... 'like this.'

Then there was Ethel. She lived in New Bridge. She was a cook at the Union-Companion boarding house. Looked more like a man than a woman. She was as tough as they come. She'd fight like a man, drink like a fish. She'd ride the cat buggy up to work. {a sled or trailer pulled by a D8 large caterpillar tractor, called the candy wagon for the supplies brought up, also bringing miners riding up to work from Cornucopia to Union portal}. She was half loaded, telling dirty stories and someone grabbed her ass. She got mad and jumped clear out of the buggy, as it was going. {there are steep cliffs in places on the narrow road up}. They all thought she'd killed herself, looking back down the trail, there she was, shaking her fist at 'em.

The last time I saw Ethel, the Chinese kitchen helper had probably grabbed her, and she was chasing him with a big knife. We treated the Chinese well, those old stories about burying them alive in the mines are lies. There were Chinese owned mining companies over in Sparta, before my time.

To get hired at the mine you had to 'rustle.' It was the art of getting known. You'd be there and try to meet the boss as every shift ended. The foreman would come out of the mine, he'd look at someone and say: 'You!,' and they were hired that way. I was rustling, at the same time painting houses in Cornucopia. I'd been rustling every day for 30 days, went up to the boss, and said: 'Could I have a day off?' No other rustlers would even speak to the boss. I {still} got the job because the boss asked me, 'you know horses?' I answered that I did, my father was a breeder. I took the bosses horse down to Halfway to breed her.

Another way to get hired was to be known by the miners, then talk to the boarding house woman and get credit to stay and eat. Called 'get on the bill.' If she thinks you're honest, you can get in. In 2 or 3 weeks, to settle the credit she's due, she'll go to the foreman and make a recommendation for hire.

In the boarding house dining room, miners had their own chairs. Married miners had houses or cabins in Cornucopia or Halfway. Most of those houses were sold and moved when the mine shut down. There was no resentment about {miners renting} the company owned cabins.

Following is an answer to a question about any spiritual aspect of working underground in a potentially deadly environment - tommy-knockers, etc.

Just jokes. Nearly all the Welsh miners were gone by the time I got there. Just the two Hunsaker brothers, I think, by the 1930's.

When Coulter was first blasted through, from below, {connecting to the Union underground workings} water started draining from old works that had been flooded. They sent one guy down the ladder for the first time in years {examining the older previously flooded levels} He didn't come back. A second guy was sent down later to find the first{bosses were asking}where are they? The third guy went down wearing a respirator. He found the two bodies, it was bad air. They got the bodies out wearing respirators. Vic and Joe Harrison had nearly new Ford V8s to take the bodies into town. We didn't think that was possible, the road as steep as it is. They spun their wheels, but made it up to the Union adit. After that, they sold a lot of Fords.

One fellow, a Greek named Joe Kippel, was riding the ore bucket down the tram {outside on the mountain}. The wind knocked a bucket from the other line into his, it threw him out. He {remains} was picked up below with a scoop shovel {the same story was told to the author by Larry Haugstad.}

The closet smelters were in Salt Lake and Rodeo, Calif., near S.F. In the late 30's we shut down the Union Mine mill, they took it down. The ore was then brought down by cat, or through the mine, to the Coulter mill.

Dale's background:

My grandparents, in 1878, came by covered wagon, over the Oregon Trail. We're the oldest family in Eagle Valley {one valley west from Pine Valley setting for Cornucopia}. We came over to America in 1630, married into the 'Mayflower family.' Our family has the only century farm in the valley. Grandma taught school and Grandfather was a rancher. He also grew melons.

I was born in 1917. I was the first 'Liberty baby' in Eagle Valley. That's the first baby born after World War 1 was declared. Granddad got a savings bond as a prize. They were taking a picture of him holding me in the air. I pissed on his head.

I had some money saved {when the mine shut down in 1942}, left mining and went into aviation school. That's why I'm still alive. I didn't see a future in mining, no promotions, safety risks. A lot of the miners went over to work the Sunshine mine in Idaho, it kept going during the war. I helped with the war effort in aviation.

My current home {see photo} was built in 1883 by Doc Howard. It was a stagecoach way station. My wife and I have three kids, grandchildren and great grandchildren.

Interview with Bonnie Herdlick
(by the author, comments used with her permission) at Pine Valley, Halfway Museum, Labor Day, 9/4/2006)

Bonnie Herdlick is a gracious, forthcoming 94 year old with a surprising memory for detail, considering her age. She was the wife of manager

Jared A. Herdlick of Cornucopia Gold Mines. Bonnie's grandparents came to Oregon in a covered wagon. When she moved up to Cornucopia in 1930, the Union Mine mill was still considered the main adit. Bonnie's father worked as a carpenter at the Union Mine. The Union Mine site, where Bonnie lived, is about two miles above the town site of Cornucopia. A large, industrial mine mill building and many other surface buildings existed, including the large cook and boarding houses. All are now gone. There is now only one small shack standing.

About 500 yards away from the Union Mine tunnel house, perched on a bluff with a commanding view of Pine Valley and the mountains across, with a view nearly into Idaho on a clear day, sat the mansion. This extensive home, near the mine, was perched on the steep eastern slopes of Cornucopia Mountain. Today, locals call the remaining foundations 'the mansion.' It was indeed a true mansion. Walking up the steep mountain road, one senses the extreme difficulty and expense the mine endured to haul massive amounts of materials up to the site, over the years: first by ox, mule, horseback and then by cat.

Bonnie's former home, the mansion, was built in 1910. It is now just foundations, some up to 12 feet high, on a grand scale. The kitchen and basement boiler room chimneys rise, castle like, fully three stories high. The third, larger, chimney contains three full hearths, also rising three stories. One imagines the great room, dining and master bedroom fireplaces burning warmly on winter nights. The miners, looking down on the mansion from the nearby rough brown plank boarding house must have been awed and probably envious of the spaciousness of the manager's house. Some flat wreckage remains today from the cook and boarding houses.

If one has visited the Sonoma Valley ruins of author Jack London's 'Wolf House,' these ruins are from the same vintage. The Cornucopia mansion is smaller than the gigantic home that London never got to live in. London's mansion-to-be was burnt in an arson fire set by an angry construction worker just as finishing touches were being applied. The extensive cement foundations remaining from London's home are similar to the mine mansion's foundations.

Bonnie explained why there is no wreckage, other than foundations, left at the site. During the depression, the mine tore down the mansion and reused the materials for mine buildings down the mountain, near the town of Cornucopia. This occurred when the Coulter tunnel was finished, far down the mountain, in 1937. The mine built new structures with the materials, including some houses in town. She did not use the term recycle. That is, apparently, exactly what Cornucopia Mines did with materials from the mansion.

To their credit, the mine did not build another manager's mansion down at the town site, in the depths of the great depression. In the then-decrepit town of Cornucopia, the construction of a new manager's mansion would likely have been viewed as inappropriate.

Bonnie helped miners solve minor medical problems. She explains what it was like living in the mansion near the Union Mine:

> I had nurses training...spent a lot of time caring for my sick child. We stayed put in the winter, there were snow drifts deeper than 20 feet. One April we still had nine feet of snow on the ground. There was a lot going on inside the house. One wing of our house was the mine's office, and another wing housed the engineers. There were lots of other buildings that served as shops and garages...We had a cook just for the house, I helped with the cleaning..... by the 1930's there was no mine doctor, there was a mine doctor there years ago, I heard, but none either down in the town {Cornucopia} or up at the mine in the 1930's, the closest doctor was in the town of Halfway... All the miners were trained in first aid, so we took care of each other. We really looked forward to the arrival of the 'candy wagon.' Came up to the mine every day.... hauling supplies for the mine, bunkhouse and some for us.... hauling miners who lived down in Cornucopia up to work...in the winter it was a large sled pulled by horses or a tractor, summer a cat {bulldozer}.
>
> Inside the mine, I got in the car {probably an empty ore car, in a train of empties pushed by a small electric locomotive, going in to be filled with ore}... went in several times.....it was lit with electric bulbs, looked bright like a city street...there's always water running out next to the tracks....about a mile in we came to the hoist {a reference to the principle, but not the only vertical shaft in the mine}....we got in the hoist and rode all the way up, inside, to the Last Chance level {a mine, by then, connected to and owned by Cornucopia Mines}....

In answer to the question 'did your husband ever have any trouble with unruly miners?'

> The men would have followed my husband anywhere, he was a good leader. We could hear the loud mine mill all the time, in the house...

the mill ran 24 hours, when even one stamp broke down, day or night, Jared could tell, he'd hear that and go over and help get it running again....

In answer to the question, "Did you hear, as the manager's wife, hear about miner resentment over anything, for example miners having to buy supplies at the company store?"

No. The company did own the main store down in Cornucopia, but the prices were kept reasonable, there were a couple of private stores {12 miles} down in Halfway with similar prices....the mine offered credit....the company helped the miners out in many ways...they blasted out a lunch room inside the Coulter Tunnel so the miners didn't have to go so far out to eat....

In answer to the question, "When most gold mines in the U.S. closed in the 1920's, how did Cornucopia Gold Mines manage to keep going during much of that time?"

I heard we were closed for several years in the 1920's. The town {below} was in pretty bad shape when we moved in...there was still good ore reachable by the tunnels...we found enough ore to keep going... they {Cornucopia Gold Mines}had bought the Red Jacket mine, reached ore from the inside ..{via Union adit} it was a good one, too...we had a good cyanide mill that recovered better, right before we left, they had nearly finished the Coulter Tunnel down below....it's cheaper to go from the bottom up.....eventually we bought the Baker Mill...the mill at the Union Companion was torn down in the early 1940's... {this explains the lack of wreckage at the massive mine mill site near the Union Mine entrance}.

In answer to: "Was there a spiritual side to working inside the earth, considering it was a dangerous job where one might die any day?"

These were good men, there was a Catholic Church down in town {Cornucopia} till the snow knocked it down. In the original mine there were Welch Cousin Jacks who had superstition, they were all gone by the time we got there, no, I never heard of ghosts in the mine...

In answer to: 'Why did you leave Cornucopia?'

We moved to Seattle, the big city! My husband was an engineer and manager for bigger mines, then, when the war broke out there was a call for engineers to find strategic metals, he worked at the big mine in Juneau, Alaska. Jared died at age 72, he was born in 1902.

Miner E.S.P.
(article, 1981, Volume 3, *Pine Valley Echoes*)

A driller reported a very unusual incident happened while he was working at the Union Mine. There are always two men who work in pairs. This one driller had a helper who left the Union Mine to go down to 'Copia and work in the Coulter Tunnel just after the tunnel had been operating for some time. They ran short of help there at the Coulter and the boss asked the driller if he would come down there and work at the Coulter Tunnel, He said 'yes.'

He then went to his partner at the Union and told him goodbye. His partner said, 'Will you be back?' He replied, 'No.' This reply mystified the driller helper, he couldn't figure him out saying that.

The very first shift this man of Swiss or Scandinavian descent (name not known), worked at the Coulter, he was killed when a round of shots was blasted. He never got away quick enough.

Excerpts from Article Titled "Freighter, Sawmill and Candy Wagon...."
(copyrighted by Sybyl Smith, Peanut Butter Publishing)

Margaret, my wife, and I moved there {to the Union Mine manager's mansion} as caretakers of the big mansion. This was where we spent most of our honeymoon.

There were three levels, two above the basement. There were four large fireplaces in the big house. The house was built in a large u shape. We estimate the cost would be about $25,000 to $35,000.

When back in 1921, I, Everett, worked in the Union Mine on the ore cars and they were pulled by one single horse, 6 to 7 cars at one time. They used 3 horses on different shifts. The horse pulled on the front and the driver rode on the back of the train and operated the brakes. Old Buck was the horse's name. You could holler at him to go and stop. He was a small work horse, weighed about 1,200 lbs. The horse was very well broke and gave us no trouble.

The {ore} cars running off the track was a very common occurrence, often in the tunnel and sometimes on the dump, a real big job to get them back on again. The boss was pretty mad if you let ore runaway over the dump....I drove the last train of ore cars loaded with ore out of the Coulter tunnel in 1941.

I worked up at 'Copia a good many years. There was only one saloon in the later years that 'Copia operated, known as the Keller Hotel. Rooms were on the second floor and the saloon down on the first floor. There were many dances with lots of fights going on then. There was a jail, but most of the ones that raised Cain were taken home, if they were able to walk.

Inside Cornucopia Mine, 1980's –
Conversations with Mine Geologist Larry Bush
(talks with the author, quoted with permission, several occasions starting October 2006)

Larry is listed in two publications as mine geologist and caretaker. According to Larry, a short new entrance adit was cut in the 1980's to bypass a cave-in at the main Coulter entrance, in order to access the network of tunnels. Ore has not been removed, beyond a small amount for sampling, since 1941. Some tunnels, Larry indicated, are partially caved or flooded. Not all levels were evaluated in the 1980's. Some working levels must be in a very dangerous state of disrepair, since most timbering stopped in 1941. Some tunnels are in untimbered hard rock, and in some tunnels the timbering rots away in time. The living rock shifts and moves through time. Mr. Bush States:

The Union shaft is now a death trap. Rotting timbers take out the oxygen. Lots of bad air in various places, we pumped air into all of the areas we worked in. Our project was clean up and assessment of value. The {going in from Coulter} mine was in good shape. Deep inside, in the compressor room, sits a large brass and iron Sullivan air compressor. There's lots of stuff in the tunnels, rotten powder boxes, etc. The hoist is still at the top of the main shaft, in from Coulter."

Because the mine was worked at different times, there's not one main shaft from top to bottom. There are three separate vertical shafts, makes the mine expensive to operate. Deeper in, where we didn't work, I touched timbers that disintegrated. I've stepped on iron mine rail tracks that turned to dust under my feet."

There was mining work we found that was on no map at all. Must have been some high-grading, {theft}...could have been after the war. We didn't get all the way up to the Union or Clark levels from Coulter, too dangerous."

---

[17] *Workingman's Dead*, Garcia, Hunter, Ice Nine Publishing.

CHAPTER 5
CHRIS SCHNEIDER - MR. CORNUCOPIA

CHRIS SCHNEIDER LABORED FOR CORNUCOPIA GOLD MINES LONGER than anyone else. Chris worked for the mines for nearly 70 years, counting his time as caretaker. Chris was given the job of mine caretaker during the early 1950's. He performed this job until the early 1970's. There were other caretakers: Charles Snedden, Olive Marker and Larry Bush. His father Chrislof migrated with other family members from Germany in 1894. Chris arrived in Cornucopia in 1897.

Schneider's father was a miner at the Union Mine, nicknamed at the time 'Old Faithful' because it kept operating when other mines had shut down. Chrislof died in a mining accident at the Union Mine in 1899, when Chris was just 14. At that time our government did not require companies to carry worker's compensation insurance. Social Security did not exist. Without income the Schneider family had to quickly start earning money. Chris' mother rented rooms and provided board to gold miners.

The Union Mine boarding house was Chris' first job station for Cornucopia mines in 1899. At the time the avalanche devastated the Queen of the West Mine, Chris was working a couple of miles away at the Union Mine. When Chris reached the age of 16, the minimum age allowed by the company, he applied for a job in the mine. Working at nearly every job at the mine; fixing mining equipment in the blacksmith shop became Chris' strength and passion. The blacksmith shop evolved into what would now be called a machine shop. At one time the mine blacksmith shop had four separate forges operating at once.

Chris' future wife, Jesse, and her family lived in Cornucopia when the population was close to 300 people. The Schneiders did not have any children. Jesse's father was killed in a 1939 mill accident. Tragically, both Schneiders' fathers were killed while working at Cornucopia Mines.

It may seem ironic that Chris dedicated most of his working life to the very companies that were involved with the death of family members. Apparently, the Schneiders were very forgiving people, holding no recorded resentment about the industrial deaths. Music had to have played a role to ease their sadness, playing was a specialty of Chris' and his family. From Germany, his father brought west a quality copy of a Stradivarius violin. Chris and his band played at the miners' dances in Cornucopia.

The music consisted of old time tunes such as: Sally Goodin, Ragtime Annie, Turkey in the Straw, Oh Susannah, and others. His sister would accompany on piano, and a nephew on sax, banjo and drums. In later years, Chris would entertain guests at their home in Cornucopia by playing the violin, accompanied by his sister on the piano. Juxtaposed with the rhythmic simplicity of Chris playing his fiddle for dancing miners were corporate owners doing a business dance, maneuvering in offices for the fiscal survival of the mine. Schneider states:

> {I}...had a lot of compliments on our music. I get a big kick out of it. ....I play the fiddle for dances, but got the banjo out last evening and amused myself playing and singing. I think my neighbors figure me bugs or something. But it's all right with me, whatever they think.[18]

At the town site of Cornucopia today, the Schneider home is the oldest and largest historic structure still in good repair. The house is framed by an ornate front porch, including the covered balcony at the front and a full length covered side porch. Chris's beautiful two story home's survival is in danger.

Chris' large back porch-shed, attached to the house and once serving as a covered bridge between the house and the still standing outhouse, has been knocked down by the weight of each winter's snow. The wreckage of the back porch structure is leaning heavily against the rear of the home, over time with deep snows, a possibly destructive condition affecting the rest of the house.

The collapsed back porch area was called 'cat heaven,' as Chris' wife loved cats. By living in and maintaining the home, since they bought it in 1900, and up into the 1970's, the Schneiders preserved the 1890's home, shoveling the roof and saving it from the crushing snow loads. Ghost town tourists were often treated by the Schneiders to coffee and dessert. Locals indicate that Chris and Jesse were really nice people, heroes of the mountain in their own way. Jesse had a beautiful flower garden, a difficult feat at that elevation.

In the 1920's the miner Chris built a log hunting lodge far up Cornucopia Mountain. Chris' cabin, a mile above and to the north-west of the Union Mine, still stands. Named 'Schneider Cabin' on maps, it is currently used by the local snowmobile club. The family's legacy also lives on via 'Schneider Meadow,' a few miles east and higher than the Cornucopia town site. The meadows are where Chris' father established a homestead prior to 1900.[19]

In the 1930's, Chris was elected mayor of Cornucopia several times, a testimony to his popularity amongst fellow miners and families. In letters to a friend, Chris writes about 'coasting' in the snow, a reference to cross country skiing or sledding. It is known that he skied, cross country, and snow-shoed. He was an active man. Chris' passion for his work, his kindness and civic leadership are all indicated in a 1940 letter. He wrote:

> I am getting younger every day hammering steel...{there is a}new company hall....a swell building, maple floor to dance on. Some class, I am thinking. I am still alone in the shop, doing the sharpening and general work. Have a helper once in a while. Phil does not seem to improve very fast." {Phil is a former miner and longtime mine blacksmith shop co-worker. Phil has 'miner's lung' or silicosis.}
>
> A big event is taking place here on the 17th, the dedication of the new company hall...starts out with a grand march, which I've been asked to lead. The company is also serving a free lunch, ice cream and coffee.....no work in the mine that evening, so everyone can attend."
>
> I attended Phil's funeral and was one of the pall bearers. I sure felt bad that he had to leave us. I have really missed him, for we were partners and worked well together.[20]

Chris left the employment of Cornucopia Mines after shut down in 1942, moving for a while to Kellogg, Idaho to work in the silver mines. He soon returned to work under maintenance supervisor Charles

Smedden, on a crew varying in size depending on the season, up to six workers for the entire mine complex.

Despite mining operations ceasing, the owners wanted to keep as many of the tunnels open and as usable as possible. After all, operations could start-up again, depending on the price of gold. If no maintenance is done, any mine will eventually fall into a condition where start up is prohibitively expensive. Rotten timbers and stopes filling up with water creates conditions where even extensive rebuilding is no longer a practical option. It was up to Smeddon, then Schneider as chief caretaker to provide mine upkeep and building maintenance with a very limited budget.

In the early 1960's, the Schneiders started living in Halfway during the winters. Chris would still travel up to the mines in mid-winter to remove snow from his house and mine building roofs. They lived in their Cornucopia home in the summers, moving full-time to Halfway in the late 1960s. Chris passed away in Halfway in 1975 at age 90.

Interview with Gold Miner David Aeder
(by daughter Janet, at his home, responding to written questions from author, May 2007)

Mr. Aeder owned and mined the Chloride Mine in western Baker County for many years. Cornucopia Mines Company hired him, in the 1950's, to help Chris Schneider with surface maintenance, and to repair the pipe system that fed their power plant on Pine Creek. The family lived in one of the 1930's Cornucopia Mines office buildings near town. David:

> We put up a new bridge across Pine Creek where the pipeline crossed the creek. I worked with Chris Schneider, Roy Pickler {former Cornucopia underground supervisor} and his son....this was water feeding the Pelton wheel at the power plant {a 6 foot high metal wheel with cups, a power generating device} water from a side creek up above on the east side of Pine Creek.
>
> One evening, the wind came up.....we were staying in one of the office buildings at the time....a tree crashed into the water line and broke it.....we all lost power...after a lot of work falling logs and winching them across the creek to service as a pipe support, we fixed the pipe....Chris drove his jeep up to turn the water back on.....I was going to set off some dynamite {as a signal} to let him know it was

OK.... he drove down anyway...the {bridge} logs spread apart under pressure.....a flange opened up...on the pipe....a great big fan of water shot up 60 feet into the air. Quite a site for the tourists up there. We fixed it and this time it held.

I bought a pneumatic stoper {drill} and some re-agents from them ...someone stole that Cornucopia stoper from the Chloride....

Conversation with Blair Smeddon
(talking with the author, used with permission, several occasions starting 10/15/2006)

Blair's father was first a miner and then placed in charge of maintenance at Cornucopia Mines after operations were stopped in 1942. His father left employment of Cornucopia Mines in 1956. Blair was born in 1935, attending, in part, grade school in the town of Cornucopia. He has been inside many of the workings of the mines, helping his father perform essential upkeep during the 1950's.

During this period, mine owners directed Smeddon to sell mine machinery for scrap iron. The machinery was obsolete, and generated income to pay for the mine's general upkeep. Chris Schneider's Cornucopia home is currently owned by the Smeddon family. Chris Schneider was the great uncle of Blair's wife Jenny. Blair kindly answered questions:

> We still worked in the Coulter Tunnel starting in the early 1950's, kept it in good shape. The Incline Raise {a name for the area mining upward from Coulter Tunnel to reach the lower levels of Union Mine} was complete. I was in high school, helping my dad. We were using the battery powered one and two ton locomotives to get around and haul timbers. My dad did a lot of re-timbering. I remember a lunch room inside the Coulter Tunnel, no kitchen. It was close to the compressor room. We didn't get too far in, there were too many slippery rocks {from above}.
>
> There was a lot of assessment work done in the 1950's to maintain ownership of nearby non-patented mining claims. The tracks ran right out of Coulter Tunnel to the blacksmith shop or the mill. The powder house was still used into the 1950's. Cornucopia Mines took the most ore out, of all the groups that ever owned the mines. They scouted other mines, sending their geologist to see if they could do well or not. The company operated out of Spokane, Washington. The workers respected the bosses. Especially in the depression, everyone was real

happy to have a job. Nobody sat around and bitched about the boss. Except there was one company mine boss in Spokane, we didn't ever meet him, who stole a bunch of money and skipped out to South America.

Cornucopia Mines was a closely held company. They didn't sell much stock. When they did, it was through {the reputable} First National Bank. I can't remember miners ever buying any stock. After work, some of the miners, during winter, would ride down the steep mountainside on scraps of corrugated metal, like sleds.... A buncha hippies bought the mine in the late 1960's, they made some money selling timber off the land....

Working with Chris Schneider – Conversation with Larry Haugstad
(by the author, with permission, at Larry's home, Halfway, 8/31/2006)

Larry worked for Cornucopia Mines in the early 1970's, part time in the winter. He was supervised by Chris Schneider, who by that time was too old to climb on roofs shoveling snow off the few remaining mine buildings.

Schneider started working for Cornucopia Mine at an early age. Most of what I have to say comes from his tales. Schneider was a great story teller. He wanted to be a gold miner from his earliest years... lots of the miners were local people. There is a story about one mine {owner} nearby who hired a bunch of Chinese workers, fell behind paying their wages, then blasted the tunnel they were working in and killed them to avoid paying wages.

Some of the miners, when they were working high grade ore, would take nuggets out in their snoose {chewing tobacco} cans.

There was a tramway to haul ore from the upper mine {Queen of the West and Last Chance} down to the mill. It took the ore down several thousand feet to the valley floor where it was hauled over to the Baker mill. Miners used to ride the buckets up and down until one of them fell out. He fell so far, they say this remains were picked up down below with a scoop shovel. From then on miners were forbidden to ride in tram buckets. Miners and wives were great gardeners in the town of Cornucopia, raised a lot of food like strawberries. The company owned the stores in Cornucopia that miners would buy supplies from.

There were two power generator plants, one for the townsite and one for the mine. Down the creek they had a dam and turbines to make power for both. The old road was on the south side of Pine creek, new road on the north side. The closest doctor was in Halfway. Ore was brought down to the railroad by wagon, later trucked from mine to Robinette, now under water.

When UNC reopened the Coulter shaft in the 1980's, they wouldn't let anyone in the shaft that wasn't working for them at the time, and I wasn't. But I knew someone who was, so I got in with him. They re-timbered a lot, maybe 5 miles of tunnel, I didn't go too far in, but far enough to go in the generator room, all in good shape. At times, we were walking in up to 1 ½ feet of water. I don't think that the lower levels are too flooded because the mine drains itself out. They worked it up from below, and from levels up above at different times. The Coulter adit is about 8 by 8 feet, one set of tracks.

---

[18] *Pine Valley Vignettes Vol. II,* Sybyl Smith, Peanut Butter Press, 1996, letters from Schneider to Della Buchanan.

[19] Lewis A. McArthur and Lewis L. McArthur, *Oregon Geographic Names,* 7th ed. (Portland: Oregon Historical Society Press, 2003), 723.

[20] Ibid.

CHAPTER 6
PHOTOS: THEN AND NOW

Avalanche at Cornucopia Mines.
Note miners and rescuers digging for survivors and victims.

Early view of Cornucopia Mines Union adit and mill buildings.

Vanner room at Cornucopia Mines mill.
The vanners concentrated gold into a slurry of gold, mercury and fine debris.

Cornucopia miners riding into the mine sitting on cars of timbers.

Cornucopia Mine, Union adit, showing mill, white waste rock dump. On lower left are two miner buildings not part of the Cornucopia Mines. On far right is the 'mansion': Union adit mine offices and managers housing.

Miners on steps of Cornucopia Mine dining hall at Union adit.
Bunkhouses in background.

4th of July holiday, miners' drilling contest in town of Cornucopia.

Postcard of Cornucopia Mine.

Cornucopia Mine, Colter Adit current view. First opened in 1935.
(Author photo.)

ABOVE: Current view of the town of Cornucopia, looking north down main street. (Author photo.) BELOW: Historical photo from same location.

The last Cornucopia miner – Dale in front of his home south west of Cornucopia. (Author Photo.)

CHAPTER 7
MINING IN CORNUCOPIA: ENVIRONMENT AND FUTURE POSSIBILITIES

GOLD MINERS AND GOLD MINES EXIST AS AN INTEGRAL PART OF the reality and the myth of the west and the old west. Gold miner vocabulary has become imbedded in our everyday language: paydirt, shaft, nuggets, drifter, pans out, glory hole, stake a claim, mother lode, bonanza and other expressions all stem from miner language. The opposite of bonanza is bust, or in Spanish: borrasca. We all talk gold miner's talk.

The Cornucopia miners and family members are a golden treasure unto themselves. In 2005, there were 2 known people alive who had worked inside Cornucopia Mines before the main shut-down in 1941. Obviously, we do not want the miners to go, they are so few, but when they do, a cycle is completed. The story of the Cornucopia Mine is, in a way, like a cycle, a time machine.

The written history of gold mining changes over time. There are thousands of books about gold mining and gold rushes, often giving repetitious stores of boom and bust. The search for gold rolled westward with the nation across Native American lands, earlier, up from the south with the Spanish. Existing Native American nations were displaced by the westward expansion. The myth of the existence of the seven golden cities of Cibola persisted in the west for nearly two centuries. Gold seekers sought a place called Golconda, a mythical land of gold and silver.

United States history books and school text books, in the past, oddly viewed the displacement of the natives in the west as a positive, practical event. In the late 1960's historians and authors started to revise the view of both the ecological and cultural ramifications of western gold mining. Clear evidence of this historical revisionist trend emerges through the reading of mining history and western history books published during the 19th, 20th and 21st centuries. The focus, the perspective, the writer's angle about gold mining changes over time.

The ancient quest for gold continues, it has not gone away, there is just less mining. New mining issues emerge. Gold mining today is most often financed by large multinational corporations. Environmental laws exist to mitigate some of the damage. Government enforcement of safety and environmental rules at the new large pit mines has been spotty. There are still hard working independent gold miners in the west, scratching a living from the earth. They have to follow the same environmental rules that the large corporations have to abide by. It is difficult, fiscally, for the small businesses to comply with government regulations. Hard feelings exist due to the conflict between an independent miner's bottom line and the expensive but necessary mining regulations set by the government.

Mining can occur that follows ecological principles; it is much more expensive, compared to the mining methods of long ago. Ore processing can now be done with cyanide in a totally contained system that creates less damage to the environment. Mines have completed extensive restoration projects on mined over land. The U.S. government declared the tailings piles Cornucopia Mines a 'superfund' toxic site, but with a rating of 'NFA' – meaning no further action. The mine owners were required to cover the tailings piles with a thick layer of crushed rock not containing any traces of cyanide or other metals, and current land owners have been ordered not to disturb the covered tailings.

There is economic value in mine tailings. In Colorado, mine tailings were used extensively as quarries of coarse gravel for home construction, roads, and unfortunately, even in school yards. These tailings contained toxic metals. There is ample government documentation of the tailings mitigation project at Cornucopia available on line, if one desires more detail.

We're aware, as are the trout in Pine Creek, of the effect of industrial discharge in fragile ecosystems. We are also aware of the right of people to use land they own, as long as it does not harm the environment as specified by law. Small mine operators are beginning to work again, both downstream on Pine Creek from Cornucopia, and near both the towns of Union and Sumter. When one speaks with local miners, they are very unhappy with governmental regulation. Speaking with environmentalists, they are not happy with the gold miners' practices.

There is hope for both a gold miner's small business surviving and compliance with environmental laws at the same time. Perhaps the hope lies in the continually rising price of gold. This trend, if continued, might allow small mines to operate and be able to comply with environmental rules. This issue has many sides, many viewpoints, and many risks.

No matter what occurs at Cornucopia the surrounding Eagle Cap Wilderness will always maintain its ancient solitude. Although it could be viewed as just a complicated hole in the ground, Cornucopia Mine still remains a virtual underground bank vault of gold. According to one engineer's estimate,[21] less than half of the deeper ore has been taken from Oregon's richest gold mine.[22]

Is it possible that the 360,000 acre Eagle Cap Wilderness, with its 540 miles of trails, and an active gold mine could exist as neighbors without any harm to the nearby wilderness? What new mining methods can be used that do not negatively affect the environment? Can mining be done that does not violate the spirit of place in the mountains? The existing treasure in Cornucopia Mines and mountains calls to us, as do the mountains.

Considering current forest uses of timber and recreation, Eagle Cap Mountains are already heavily used, during summer, by humans, but at the same time independent of humans, as they have been for infinitely longer than we have walked on them. The enigmatic mask we call mountains hide their gold deep. We are somehow drawn to the mountains. Sacred mountains, rearing solidly aloft, as Cornucopia's glistening peak was surely sacred to the natives, as are Oregon's Mt. Jefferson, Mt. Fuji, Denali, Shasta, Popocateptl in Mexico and Kilimanjaro in Africa.

In Cornucopia's deep clefts and rugged grey and white speckled granite cliffs, below bright green forested slopes of white fir, lies a mystery. It is a riddle to be solved, or left alone. In the strata of the earth is a mineral, great and invisible from the surface. It is gold. A standard of value, pure gold contains many colors; yellow, pink and red. Gold is used as a metaphor for purity and generosity. Enigmatic gold, one of the primordial powers of our planet. Gold, glinting like the sun of life in the earth. Cornucopia, the myth, the mine, the miners, the village, and the mountain stake their own claims in one's consciousness.

---

[21] *Oregon's Golden Years*, Miles F. Potter 1976 page 154.

[22] Numerous pages in the University of Wisconsin's document statistics on Cornucopia's status of largest mine in Oregon, from: Ecology and Natural Resources Collection, University of Wisconsin: digital.library.wisc.edu/1711.dl/EcoNatRes. Also, communications with info@friendsofthedredge.com confirms that all three Sumpter Dredges did not produce near the total amount of gold compared to Cornucopia Mines.

Afterword

GOING TO CORNUCOPIA TODAY TAKES ONE UP A WELL GRAVELED, improved road on the east side of Pine Creek, north from Halfway, Oregon. Any car can navigate the road to the town site, when the snow is gone. Bootlegger's grade is unmarked. On the left side of the road, off through the trees, across Pine Creek, one notices the Bonnanza (named with two n's) placer mine, operating from the 1980's, a few miles downstream from Cornucopia Mines. There is a wide, green buffer zone between the Bonnanza mine and the creek.

Just before the town and mine site, the road takes a sharp U turn, after a turnoff to the right going to the wonderful, new Cornucopia Lodge. This fine lodge, with a stunning view of the mountains of Eagle Cap Wilderness and an adjoining horse pack station, are the only businesses currently operating in the old mining town. Like the old west, the economy includes lodging and horses.

The historic Cornucopia town site begins suddenly at the sharp curve crossing Pine Creek, the road heading south and slightly down hill back on the west side of the creek. On a ramble through the town, one can sense the past glory of the town, perhaps the spirit of Cornucopia. Coming into the town site for the first time, perhaps you possess sepia toned photos in your imaginary landscape. The vivid colored landscape of the ghost town emerges and blends with the here and now.

In the town site, to the right, is a side road leading about one quarter mile up to the nearby Coulter adit and Cornucopia Mine mill site. There are a few newer vacation cabins in the area. The private property, posted 'keep out' mine site requires permission to visit. There is wreckage, extensive foundations, a few older mining buildings and the large early 1980's mine mill industrial building, incomplete inside. Even though deep and huge cement foundations of the original mine mill buildings are intact and close to the new mill building, UNC oddly elected to construct their mill structure on new cement foundations.

Considering historic mine photos of both the Union and Coulter mill complexes, it's hard to grasp that there is little left standing of all the extensive mine buildings but a 1930's cement dynamite bunker, a shop building near the Coulter adit, and a couple of shacks of unknown age. Below the mill site, settling ponds required by the government have been excavated to catch toxic water runoff from the Coulter mill site tailing piles, before the runoff enters Pine Creek.

The tailings piles were found to contain "arsenic... above EPA's criteria, lead is close to unacceptable levels." The tailings from Baker Mill site (on the east side of Pine Creek, upstream 1/2 mile) were moved to combine with the lower tailings pile and covered with non-tailings crushed rock, all on the east side of Pine Creek. Natural vegetation has now begun to grow on some of the sides of the carefully shaped tailings piles; the cycle of recovery has begun.

In the middle of what was once the town site, there are about a half dozen privately owned 1930's or earlier miners' cabins still in good repair, likely used as vacation cabins. The once thriving village has become small. What is it about a ghost town that is so fascinating? A ghost town image exists in the mind's eye, reinforced by movies, as a place where the miners and citizens suddenly moved away when they heard of a richer strike.

In the mythical ghost town, you swing open the creaky wooden saloon doors. Left behind are the poker cards, chips, and whiskey bottles on the saloon tables, now covered by dust. Mosey up to one of the tables, uncork the bottle, wipe off the dust and take a pull. Whiskey does not deteriorate with age. There is such a ghost town called Bodie, California. Much was left in Bodie when the gold miners fled. It was largely preserved when the state, long ago, bought the entire town to create a state historic park.

No such luck in Cornucopia. It is an odd, disturbing and profound notion that emerges, standing smack dab in the middle of the site of the town of Cornucopia; there is little town left. Just silence. Wait, coming through the mountain mist looks like Ben, Hoss, Adam and Little Joe, walking down the ghost town dirt street towards you. It couldn't be the Cartwrights. Virginia City was a silver mining town, not a gold mining town like Cornucopia. The mist clears, no ghosts.

The town site evokes a feeling of solitude. During an era prior to the ugliness of strip-malls, Cornucopia was an authentic wooden frontier-town. With a commercial row of businesses, some with classic second story 'false fronts' on both sides of the road, the town had ample horse parking in front of each business. The old west lived here, miners drank and fought, many good deeds and a few bad deeds were done. The town is surrounded by a now restored lush Pine forest, several varieties, plus Aspen, Tamarack and other tree species.

Perched on the hillside of the west side of the road, amongst the trees, in the middle of the town site is the last remaining historic commercial building in Cornucopia. It is a tower of Pisa-leaning two story ten bedroom boarding house from gold mining days. How long it stands will depend on the current owners' fiscal decision whether or not to shore up and straighten the structure. The windows and doors are all smashed out, letting snow blow in to severely warp the floors. Wallpaper peels from the walls, mouse droppings are scattered on the floors. Perhaps there is more we might do to encourage preservation, before the boarding house tumbles to the ground. The last business building from mining days, what can we do to save it before it totters over?

One of the privately owned lots contains the historic town jail, now boarded up and not looking like a jail at all.

A suggested donation address is specified in the appendix, if you want to help save what's left of the town. Most of the profits from this book will be donated to the Halfway Museum for a historic preservation fund for Cornucopia.

At the southernmost edge of the town site sits Chris Schneider's beautiful 1890's vintage house. It is complete with gingerbread trim and historic outbuildings, all, like most of the town, on private property. The family, thankfully, has kept the house up. Walking up to the front door and knocking, I didn't really expect Chris Schneider to greet me and tell mining tales, on account of his being dead for nearly thirty years. I had hoped that someone would be there to tell me more about life in Cornucopia. No one was home. I went straight back, on the front walk, to the road, resisting the temptation to look around, as this is clearly private property.

I felt a sudden and sharp urge to do something positive to alleviate pervasive vandalism. Where did that feeling come from, in this ghost town? So much in the town has been ruined by vandals. Lying on the ground to the side of the Schneider path, right on the edge of the road, was a carved white wooden fence gate post. The other post, on the opposite side of what once was a gate, was still standing. I placed the fallen post back upright in its original place, bracing it with rocks.

Signs clearly posted in privately owned areas indicate that tourists have not respected the property rights of current owners. Some bad apples have stolen cultural artifacts vital to the history of the town. If only each tourist did just one good deed towards preservation, and took nothing away but photos, some of the damage to the suffering town might be reversed.

On one visit to Cornucopia, I slept on the gold laced earth, mixed with some mine tailings, at the edge of the town, on U.S. Forest Service land, forming a physical and kinetic connection with the labor of the miners. Close to my camp was one of three historic miner's log cabins. If the metal roofs hold and vandals do no further damage, two of these historic log cabins should not be in danger of collapsing.

Next to the Schneider property flows Jim Fisk Creek, forming the National Forest boundary. This is the creek that mostly flows from the Union adit far above the town below Cornucopia Peak.

As one sits in the Alpen-glow evening light, pondering the town and the nearby mine, Cornucopia serves up a weird juxtaposition of the present and the antique. A potentially dangerous drug, nostalgia is. With a lawn chair, notebook and a supply of Jim-Fisk-Creek-chilled Oregon micro-brewery beer, during a couple of hours on a warm summer Saturday late afternoon and early evening, I observed exactly nine cars slowly passing through the ghost town, turning around beyond the Schneider home and heading back down towards Halfway. Once the tourist cars reached the Schneider home, continuing down the road another 100 yards, they seemed to have determined there is little left of the town. In a sense they are right.

None of the tourists observed dared to get out of their cars and look around in the town. Perhaps TV shows back at their hotel rooms were beckoning them. It appears they all left Cornucopia with metaphoric gold pans empty. To come to a ghost and miss out on all the rich organic smells and sounds of the forest is an inexplicable misfortune. Having perhaps seen historic photos of the town's business district, the tourists no doubt wondered, 'Where did the town go?' Cornucopia exists, specter-like, mostly unseen, but still present. It takes imagination and investigation of remaining stone foundations to recreate the town in the geography of the mind. Time and snow weigh heavily upon the site. Cornucopia's spirit of place remains; one just needs silence and taking time to fleetingly feel it. Could miner, teamster and shopkeeper spirits, if they remained in the ghost town in the tiniest ways, possibly feel the tourists come and go?

The next day, up the horrible rocky road that starts at the town site below, I hiked to Union adit, and then on up to Last Chance adit. The Union Mine site is a steep two miles plus hike up Cornucopia Mountain. The Union, Clark, Coulter, and Last Chance adits that so many hard working miners went to work through for so many years are collapsed. Significant flows of water issue from both Coulter and Union adits. The ice cold, clear water runs right out with buried mine car rails that mysteriously emerge from the mountain itself.

I poked around the tailings pile with my hiking staff. The Union adit was close, now. A geode thunder egg, cleaved in half, half buried in the tailings, revealed its treasure to me. There were a couple of tiny broken sea-bed fossils in the tailings pile. More treasure. The earth's equilibrium maintains, where mountains crumble away to the sea, then sea floors rise and thrust up into new mountains. Humankind occupies such a tiny slice of geologic time. We play around, for a short time, tourists on the surface of this ancient earth.

Nearly at the Union adit (mine entrance) tall bushes and pine seedlings crowd the trail. Even though I seemed to be walking along on top of an old tailings pile, the mountain was making efforts to heal itself from the ravages of mining. There was a disturbing crashing in the shrubs nearby.

Oddly enough, Bigfoot sprang to mind. I had seen no one since leaving the town site, now a few miles up the steep Jim Fisk Creek canyon. In the summer of 1996, according to the Bigfoot Researchers Organization, a family of six campers had all spotted the hairy beast lurking near the town of Cornucopia. Two of the children had a clear full body viewing. My current location was far more remote than the possible Bigfoot sighting location down at the town site.

Bigfoot it was not. The din was two children making their way, carrying water buckets. They had not been talking, so I had no clue that it was humans. Near the Union adit (mine) an extended family of hunters were camping at a level switchback in the middle of the jeep road, just above foundations of the Union Mine bunkhouse.

This small group I encountered were about to draw drinking water from the stream issuing directly from the adit, right at the mine car rails. I asked the mom, when she approached, if it was safe for her small children to drink mine-shaft water. Imagine the crumbling outhouse stations still inside, the tons of dynamite used over the century, there in the Union adit. Down the mountain; the documented high chemical levels of lead, arsenic, mercury and cyanide remain in the tailings piles. She wasn't worried at all, indicating the family had camped at the Union adit several times, and suffered no apparent health problems as a result of drinking the mine water. She told me that "the view was killer" from their camping place. It was. I hope it isn't more than the view that is killer. The group was camped a long stone's throw from the foundations of the mansion and mine cookhouse.

There on Cornucopia Mountain one can still peer deep into the mine shaft darkness through a four square foot opening, the mostly collapsed Union adit. Squeezing oneself through that grim, partly flooded portal to get a look at the underground workings is a terrible, fleeting temptation, but would most likely be a fatal, final stunt. No one should ever reenter the Union adit in its current state. Is it a tomb, or perhaps a sacred place? If one made the big mistake of crawling inside the mine, if a cave in didn't kill you, bad air surely would.

Later in the day, down the mountain from the mine, I was tramping heavily towards camp at the Cornucopia town site. This glorious day of exploration had stretched itself to my physical limits. Dinner and rest were calling. The sun was starting to set golden and orange after a strenuous hike further up Cornucopia Mountain to the Last Chance Mine. I was dead tired from scrambling up the mountain in a fruitless effort to find any remnants beside tailings piles at the Last Chance site. To get to the site of the Queen of the West would have been three more miles one way, too steep, much too far. On the road, in the dusk, one of the hunters kindly paused his battered pickup and offered me a ride down to the town site.

After getting in his truck, I learned, to my distress, from his mumblings, that he was headed down to Halfway on a beer run. He stated that they thought they had brought a large enough stash of beer, but they had consumed all of it. Alcohol and guns, for some hunters and even gold miners, is standard outdoor recreational equipment. After all, this combination is a northeast Oregon tradition of sorts going back as early as the fur trappers coming through from the 1820s to the 1840s. Nothing new, here. As we hurtled down the rough mine road, unsecured hunting gear flew around inside the pickup cab like crazed bats.

And you know that notion of the mine cook leaping from the moving mine truck, the 'candy wagon,' perhaps at that very spot, just crossed my mind. My name is Cook. Remember the cook, described by miner Dale Holcomb, jumping out? Is this a sign that I should jump out? In a beat up, stoved-in high center four wheel drive rig, the drunk driver-engineer, let's give him the mythic name Casey Jones, and I bumped and lurched too fast down that grisly steep road. The road is replete with boulders and wash-outs, along with the ghosts of miners, so long ago. Trouble ahead, on the very route that dead miners were carried down to town, trouble behind at the mine. The ride was so rough that even with a seat belt on my head slammed into the cab roof several times.

Truly a Disneyland roller coaster adventure, except the ride had authentic scenery. With relief I got out, two goose eggs poking through my hair, at the edge of the townsite, tourist knuckles white. Ah, the safety of my mountain base camp, safe with the ghosts in a ghost town. After catching my breath, I pondered; will what's left of the town survive continued use by all of us?

The future of Cornucopia likely involves exactly what is going on there right now: the lodge, hiking, horseback riding, hunting, fishing, cross country skiing, snowmobiling, mountain biking and other forms of recreation. According to the U.S. Forest Service map of the area, there are 53 high mountain lakes nearby, accessed by hiking or horseback riding up steep-walled valleys formed by ancient glaciers.

It is probable that the corporate mining days, here, are finished. To prospect on U.S. Forest Service land requires a "Notice of Intent," and operating mechanized equipment requires a "Plan of Operation" that can cost $50,000 to create and then revise at additional expense to obtain needed governmental approval. Mines also must post an initial bond with a beginning cost of $25,000, with required bond costs escalating depending on the size and scope of the operation. These mandated fees are so that potential environmental damage will not be on the taxpayer's bill. This sounds fair for larger corporations. The mine owners, all of us that visit, and those that live near Cornucopia can all help shape the future of this beautiful valley.

One can view an image of Cornucopia Peak and surrounding mountains in the distance on the City of Halfway's online webcam. Although impossible to distinguish the Union Mine site exactly in the distant mountain view, the mine is somewhere in the web camera's field of vision. One hundred years ago, imagine a gold miner's wonderment, if they could learn that their remote mine would be viewable worldwide, on a camera taking pictures every few seconds, each and every day.

Journeying on a pilgrimage to mine gold mining history, the present moment emerges, concurrent with the experience of the environment where events occurred long ago. The lure of gold, the very first mineral mentioned in the Bible, is also mentioned in Buddhist and Muslim literature. It's a huge challenge, perhaps impossible, to detect the golden heart that beats so faintly within the rock. So many gold prospectors have tried. We are all prospectors, tourist seekers in a time dualistic sense. Do we find what we expected? Perhaps the history, the gold we seek, is already inside us, in our families and in the mountains right now.

LETTER[23]

October 3, 1919, from CORNUCOPIA MINES COMPANY

Soldiers' and Sailors' Commission
of the State of Oregon
Portland, Oregon

Gentlemen:

As we are very badly in need of common labor at our mines, situated in Baker County, Oregon, we desire to place the following information at your disposal, in hope that it may help you in sending us men:

We have two gold mines and the class of labor we need is unskilled, the work to be performed is shoveling and tramming underground. The wages are $4.00 per day for eight hours, we charge $1.00 per day for board and room, but the men are supposed to furnish their own blankets. There is opportunity for advancement to better positions, such as mining and timbering, which pays $4.50 and $5.00 and there is also an opportunity to contract the work which pays from $4.50 to $6.00 per day with the minimum of $4.00 guaranteed[.] In some places the mines are wet but in such places rubber coats are furnished by the company, to protect the men from the drip.

Fares will be advanced to the men and deducted from their pay checks after they have gone to work.

Very truly yours,

CORNUCOPIA MINES COMPANY

P.S. Keep on sending men until notified to stop.

---

[23] From http://arcweb.sos.state.or.us/exhibits/war/intro/postwar.html

SOURCES

Gold Mining in Oregon, Bert Webber, 1995 ISBN 0-936738-77-4

Oregon's Golden Years, Miles F. Potter 1976 ISBN 0-87004-254-8

University of Oregon, Knight Library, Oregon Collection: 2 boxes of ledgers and letters, records from Cornucopia Mines

University of Utah, Marriott Library, box 35 XOP, fd #s 16 and 17

Author's collection of over 800 timecards, requisitions and shift reports by Cornucopia Mines, 1937 to 1940

Newspaper article: *Baker City Herald*, March 14, 1904

Oregon State Department of Geology and Minerals, H. Brooks and L. Ramp, State of Oregon publication, 1968

Ghost Towns of the Pacific Northwest, Lambert Florin, Promontory Press 1970

"The Cornucopia Gold Mine of N.E. Oregon," Jim Epling (unpublished thesis) available: Eastern OR University Library

Cracker Creek Museum of Mining: www.sumpteroregongold.org

WARNING

Do not enter mines. Falling rock, sudden deep openings and bad air can all be fatal.

ABOUT THE AUTHOR

Thomas Cook's articles have appeared in publications such as Roseburg, Oregon's *News Review*. This is his first book. He is a retired educator and counselor living in Eugene, Oregon.

Please send donations to:

Cornucopia Preservation Fund
Care of: Pine Valley Community Museum
P.O. Box 673
Halfway, OR 97834

CPSIA information can be obtained
at www.ICGtesting.com
Printed in the USA
BVHW051706040123
655564BV00014B/743